AIKIDO INSIGHTS

Essays on the Intangible Aspect
of Aikido Training

H. Hoa Newens

Copyright 2010 by H. Hoa Newens

All rights reserved.

The text and illustrations in this book may not be reproduced in any format or medium without written permission from the author.

Artwork by Kori Farrell

ISBN 978-0-557-78461-5

Printed in the United States of America

Contents

Dedication		i
Acknowledgments		iii
Forewords		v
1	Set a Training Plan	1
2	Growing Through Aikido Training	3
3	Aikido as the Ultimate Martial Art	7
4	I Wanted Them to See Where They Are Going	13
5	What Aikido Does to You	19
6	How Aikido Training Reduces Violence	23
7	A Perspective on Self-defense	29
8	What Makes Aikido Aikido	35
9	Writing About Aikido Is Part of Aikido Training	41
10	Hard Training and Soft Training	45
11	Prepaid Luck	51
12	The Power and Techniques of Focusing	55
13	On Kata Practice	63
14	Service as Part of Aikido Training	69

15	Life is Conflict	73
16	From Conflict to Harmony	77
17	Saito Sensei's Legacy	83
18	The Art of Peace	89
19	Things Get Worse Before They Get Better	97
20	Dojo Expansion and Dojo Spirit	101
21	Fitness, Aikido and Tai Chi	105
22	Square Pegs, Round Holes	109
23	When Am I Ready to Teach?	115
24	Kihon Waza	123
25	Yawarakai Waza	127
26	Forty-year Lessons	131
27	Women in Aikido	137
28	Ranks in Aikido	143
29	The Mystery of Basics	149
30	How Correct Aikido Ukemi Promotes Health	155
31	First Rei, Then Waza	159
Epilogue		167
Glossary of Japanese Terms		169
About the Author		173

Dedication

This book is the coalescence of my forty-four years of Aikido training. I dedicate it to the youth of the world, including my sons Richard and Ryan. It is my hope that the insights recorded herein will help to illuminate the path of their life journeys.

H. Hoa Newens

Acknowledgments

I owe an enormous debt to the Aikido teachers who guided my growth in Aikido. They were, in chronological order, Canh Bui Sensei, Phong Dang Sensei, Seiichi Sugano Shihan (deceased), Bruce Klickstein Sensei, Morihiro Saito Shihan (deceased) and William Witt Shihan. Their teachings led me to the understanding that I share with the readers in this book. I am much honored to have Witt Shihan write a foreword for this book.

I am also inspired by the many friends and students in the Aikido community who gave selflessly of themselves on the mat, providing me with the experience to write this book.

I am particularly grateful to Bruce Donehower for his counsel on this project and for his foreword to this book; and to Bill Martin for sharing valuable advice. Many heartfelt thanks are due to Kori Farrell for providing the illustrations in the book and to Toby Hargreaves for proof-reading.

And of course, no project of this scale would be successful if I did not have the total support of my family, including my parents, Phillip and Madeleine Newens and my wife Phoebe. My father provided invaluable counsel that will outlast this project.

H. Hoa Newens
November 2010

"The secret of Aikido is to harmonize ourselves with the movement of the universe and bring ourselves into accord with the universe itself. He who has gained the secret of Aikido has the universe in himself and can say, "I am the universe."

Morihei Ueshiba O-Sensei

Foreword by Bruce Donehower

I first heard about Hoa Newens Sensei while circumambulating Mt. Tamalpais with an aikido friend from Sacramento. Sensei, at the time, had relocated from Oakland to Davis with his wife Phoebe and sons Richard and Ryan. During the hike around the mountain in Marin, my friend told me he had been practicing with Sensei at his home in Davis, where a living room had been converted for mat space. I was a bit surprised, and I thought: anyone this serious about aikido bears investigation. Little did I know. A few months later when Sensei opened his first dojo in Davis on Second Street, I attended the grand opening celebration. Sensei's depth of character, his quiet integrity, impressed me immediately. I observed a gentleman of tact, deep understanding, undeniable skill, good humor, equanimity, and dedication. I found his level of technical expertise daunting and inspiring, and I understood at once that my friend was right: this was a teacher I needed to study with.

Over the years that I have been privileged to work with Sensei, those first impressions have been repeatedly confirmed. Persons desiring to assess Sensei's technical acumen can readily do this, of course, by viewing his instructional series of aikido DVDs, which give a thorough orientation to both open-hand techniques and aiki weapons. But it is not this side of Sensei that I wish to highlight in this brief preface. Rather, I want to draw attention to a less visible side of Sensei's art.

Time and again, in his quiet way, Sensei has drawn the dojo students' attention to his belief that we should engage our minds intellectually with the art of aikido in addition to dedicating ourselves to strenuous physical practice. One way to do this, Sensei mentions, is to write about aikido and to make this intellectual activity part of our training. As I have heard him explain, this writing activity serves a dual purpose. It first allows us to reflect upon the art in a disciplined manner conducive to new insights; but secondly, it allows others a glimpse into how each of us as an individual strives to master the Way.

By emphasizing the benefits of writing about aikido, Sensei has made me more aware of a basic principle of our practice: the mind leads; the body follows. This basic principle of aiki is in its own quiet way at the heart of the mystery of what we are about.

The essays that are included in this volume thus provide inspiration for our own reflections on practice as well as insights into the inner world of an artist of the Way. They were written over a period of years for the students' newsletters at the Oakland dojo and the Davis dojo. They were meant to explain various aspects of aikido practice and are valuable to students for this reason. Aikido is a performance art – alive in the moment. Essays, however, are small markers of self-reflection that we can trace and retrace to understand better all that we experience in the living, evanescent moment of technique.

Bruce Donehower

Foreword by William Witt Shihan

Hoa Sensei appeared in my life gradually. At first he was a student at the Aikido Institute in Oakland. He began to appear more and more at other aikido functions and finally went to visit my teacher, Saito Morihiro Shihan, in Iwama, Japan. What impressed me most about him was his dedication to training—to perfecting himself. Until we became better acquainted, I did not realize how extensive his training had been. He never mentioned his background to me, and I only saw his expertise quietly and modestly displayed in the dojo. As we became friends, I began to appreciate how his aikido experience seemed to give him deeper insights to some of the issues confronting us when we were beginning the Takemusu Aikido Association. Suffice it to say, when he speaks, I listen.

This book is different than most aikido books in that it is not about technique but contains essays of thoughts we all have about our training as we progress in the art: Is it a fighting method? Will I get hurt? Why do some people call it the "non-violent" martial art? In a traditional dojo, an uchideshi, a live-in student, has the instructor to guide him, and a good instructor takes care to answer some of these questions either directly or indirectly. Most of the answers we seek come with training, however. When we are no longer with our instructor, we still develop questions and learn to answer them ourselves. We use the realm of the dojo and the training methods to gain experience in teaching, and we refine our understanding of aikido as we age.

This collection of essays is a guide to greater understanding of the martial art we call Aikido. It seeks to let the beginner know there are basic questions to be answered. The experienced student will see there is more to learn than technique. The advanced student or teacher will appreciate the intangible instruction that must be a part of every student's education. It is intended as a guide of what might be. If the reader knows what is coming, it is not difficult to meet a confrontation with a calm mind. Understanding these essays will help the aikido practitioner meet those mental hurdles we all must overcome in our life long training.

William Witt, Shihan
President
Takemusu Aikido Association

1
Set a Training Plan

Over the years I noticed that there are some students who would take off for weeks, return to the dojo to attend a few classes and a seminar then go off again. To every one of them I gave this same lecture.

If your goal is to learn Aikido, coming to class only when you feel like it is not going to get you far, or anywhere.

Personal growth involves making a leap from one level of consciousness to another level. This leap requires a lot of energy, mostly for eradicating old habits and learning new ways. Fortunately, Aikido practice, if done correctly, generates energy. This energy can be accumulated until it reaches a sufficient level to fuel the leap.

Alternatively, it can be used to fulfill mundane needs or it can be dissipated for pure relief.

After an intense Aikido *gasshuku*, you have the choice to channel the increase in energy toward more training in the dojo or longer work hours in the office. You can also squander it all at an all-night party.

It is your choice; and the decision depends on what you want from Aikido and whether you have made plans to get what you want. If you are not clear on what you want or have not made plans, then your habits take over and the energy may be wasted if these habits are not goal-oriented.

AIKIDO INSIGHTS

Effective Aikido training requires a plan for practice. This plan should include regular class attendance (three times a week is the norm); participation in special events and seminars; helping others take their tests; and helping with dojo chores. The training sessions should be regular and close enough so that their cumulative effect results in a build-up of energy.

In this respect, it is better to train every other day of the week for one hour each time than training once a week and taking a full day seminar per month.

Remember that Aikido training generates energy, which will be wasted over time if not saved and reinvested.

December 14, 1995

2
Growing Through Aikido Training

If I'm not interested in fighting, self-defense or even conflict resolution is there something in Aikido for me? I was once asked by a discerning prospective student. My answer was that it will help her grow as a human being. Here is how it works.

Whatever goal a person has set for herself in Aikido, an understanding of the effect of correct training will help to further this goal.

Let's just assume that the student's goal relates to personal growth. A person is normally not aware of the growth process that he or she is going through. Often, we know that we have grown only from hindsight and by noticing that our perspectives with regard to certain experiences have changed. For example, what was a dreadful or overwhelming experience before may now appear to us as a normal life process. Breaking up with a first love may mean the end of the world to someone who is struggling through the experience. Twenty years later, looking back, he would probably simply classify that experience as a necessary process, among other more powerful experiences that are part of growing up.

This change in perspective comes from a change in vantage point caused by an expansion of the boundaries of our awareness. This growth process can be left to the natural but haphazard processes of life - the lazy man's way to enlightenment - or can be methodically cultivated. Such cultivation is usually accomplished through a disciplined path, a well-defined and focused way of life - such as the practice of Aikido. This more focused approach can get one out of the karmic wheel faster.

The fact is that the proper practice of Aikido generates energy that can be stored and converted into consciousness. If this basic principle is not understood, a person can practice Aikido for a long time and deplete rather than increase her stock of energy. Or, the practitioner may increase her energy and squander it instead of storing it. Or, she can generate energy and store it but direct it to destructive purposes instead of nourishing her consciousness.

The first part of this principle explains that when Aikido is practiced properly it is invigorating. When a student feels drained out as a result of doing Aikido, he should stop and check his training. Perhaps he is not listening to the body and is over-exerting it. Perhaps his practice consists of doing too wide a range of techniques instead of being based on a core set of basic techniques. In this regard, a thousand times of the same move are worth more than a thousand different moves. Or perhaps, the techniques are not done correctly, that is, in such a way that maximizes energy circulation in the body.

The second part of the principle states that energy that is generated from practicing Aikido should be saved and accumulated otherwise it will be lost. The best way to accumulate this energy is to continually reinvest it in practice. In this regard, going to class three times a week on a regular basis is worth more than attending sporadic intensive seminars. Too long a time lapse between practice sessions will cause energy loss.

The third part of the principle states that one can choose where to direct the stock of energy accumulated from training. One can use this surplus energy to satisfy mundane needs, enhance sensual pleasures, procreate, destroy, pursue intellectual goals, or propel oneself further along the Aiki path. This latter choice will automatically cause an upward displacement of one's vantage point that will allow one to see more and with more clarity. Thus, one grows.

March 1, 1996

AIKIDO INSIGHTS

3

Aikido as the Ultimate Martial Art

I have read and heard a multitude of opinions about the merit of Aikido and how it compares with other well known martial arts. Most of these opinions focus narrowly on the physical aspect of the art and miss the real point of Aikido. I explain below how Aikido transcends the common concept of martial art.

A martial art is an art in which the practitioner learns ways to deal effectively with some sort of aggression whether in a defensive or offensive mode. Many such arts are based on a common fundamental principle: eliminate the source of perceived opposition to preserve the self.

This principle has its roots in the natural animal instinct to fight for survival. It causes a snake to bite at you when you step on it; it causes you to slap at the mosquito biting at your arm. It is a natural reflex.

There are also a few martial arts that are based on a principle that transcends the survival instinct and is subscribed to by more consciously evolved beings. This principle is based on the understanding that all individual selves are an integral part of a larger being and that each self is preserved by protecting the larger being. In a martial art based on this principle any aggression is viewed as a temporary imbalance and dealt with in such a way as to restore balance in the larger being. Aikido is such a martial art.

Aikido as a Self-defense Art

In the most mundane meaning of self-defense, as in defense against a mugger in the streets, Aikido is a very effective way to remove the opposition. The first move of any Aikido technique is to connect with the opponent's center through an *atemi*. In normal Aikido practice such an *atemi* is delivered so that the opponent is not physically hit but is used only to extend an energy bridge to the opponent's center. If there is a need, that *atemi* can be physically extended to impact the opponent at his most vulnerable area, his central nervous system which spans from the crown of the head to the perineum.

In addition, the Aikido student is taught at an early stage a skill that is of primary importance in many self-defense situations: the art of *ukemi*, that is, the art of receiving a technique and taking a safe fall on the ground. An average person would feel helpless when taking a hard fall on the ground. At a certain level of proficiency, the Aikido practitioner would, after connecting with the opponent as described above, get off the line of attack, receive the oncoming force then redirect it into a joint lock, throw or ground-pin, without having to destroy the opponent. It takes several years of practice, though, to reach this skill level at which the adept has transcended the natural hit-back-or-flee reflex.

Time is therefore the only drawback for taking up Aikido training as a primary self-defense method. At the highest level of self-defense, the practitioner would be in constant connection with his surroundings and would be aware of the aggressive intent before it manifests as a physical attack. Therefore, he would be able to pre-empt the attack by neutralizing this negative intent at the outset.

Aikido as a Conflict Resolution Art

On a broader level, Aikido is an art of resolving conflict, albeit conflict of a more urgent and personal type than suggested in the term "conflict resolution". Self-defense as described above is then a resolution of a specific type of conflict: physical conflict between the self and others. Aikido can also be used to resolve conflicts within oneself, conflicts among others and non-physical conflicts.

Aikido helps a person to resolve conflict by providing a way for him to blend his energy with others' in a focused manner. A conflict normally involves at least two forces colliding against each other because at least one of them has separated from the greater harmony. Aikido provides a means for one of these forces or a third party which is anchored in the great harmony to connect with the separatist, align with it and lead it back to the fold.

The Aiki force in the above scenario would have to be anchored in the great harmony. That is, first, it has to have great humility and constantly remember that it is part of a greater whole; that the opposing force is also part of that same greater whole; and that destroying the opposing force is detrimental to the greater whole. Second, it must recognize that the only movement that would benefit it is one that is in unison with the greater whole. Third, when it moves, it has to move with conviction and in a focused manner in order to lead the opposing force. If it lacks conviction or focus, it may not be able to preserve its integrity or the other force may not follow.

One can imagine the numerous applications that this principle has in our daily life.

Aikido as a Martial Art

Aikido is more than just a conflict resolution method. It is something that is not restricted by the rational thinking that underlies most "methods". It is an art, and like all arts, it takes a lifetime to master and yet it makes the master feel inadequate after a lifetime of practice. The more one practices Aikido the more one realizes its vastness and soon it becomes one's way of life.

Beside being an art, Aikido is a "martial" art. It is not an art that one practices leisurely. It is an art that one practices seriously because it affects one's well-being in an urgent manner. Aikido must be practiced with a sense of urgency, as if one's life depends on it. If it is deprived of this element, Aikido is just a pastime.

In addition, Aikido is not just any martial art. It is a non-violent martial art in the sense that it does not require the use of extreme or sudden force. An Aikido move can be intense and powerful, but involves a harmonious connection among the forces at work and fluid, not disconnected, motion. The non-violence of Aikido has nothing to do with morality and should not be mistaken for Gandhi's non-violence.

Another distinguishing characteristic of Aikido is that it cannot be practiced competitively. True competition cannot exist in Aikido because Aikido is based on the premise that both the forces at play co-exist in the same camp: one has gone astray; the other is leading it back to camp. Competition would go against this symbiosis.

Aikido as the Ultimate Martial Art

Aikido gets directly to the essence of martial arts: it allows one to preserve oneself while also preserving the surroundings in which one lives.

The student of Aikido learns to be aware of energy flows, to blend with oncoming energy and to redirect it without crushing it. All Aikido techniques are designed for this effect.

The constant repetition of the same movements over the years help to ingrain the Aikido principles explained at length above, first into the physical body, then the mental body, and finally the spiritual body of the student.

One can expect that this process takes a long time but yields permanent and broad impact on one's life, beyond the realm of many other more popular martial arts. In fact, Aikido lags in popularity mainly because it does not provide quick and tangible benefits. It foregoes all the glamour and takes the serious student directly to the essence of all martial arts.

All martial arts ultimately lead to the understanding of the principle which pervades all Aikido techniques: all individual selves are part of a greater being; the well being of each self is best preserved by protecting the welfare of the greater being. As the Founder said, "The source of *budo* is God's love - the spirit of loving protection for all beings".

In this way, Aikido is the ultimate martial art. Not to brag about, but to share with the rest of the world.

December 1, 1996

4

I Wanted Them to See Where They Are Going

The instructors and advanced students used to perform an annual demo at the dojo for the public. One year, I noticed that one of the adult students brought his two children to watch the demo and show them what they could aspire to do in the future. I thought that was a wonderful way to inspire the kids in their Aikido training.

On an overcast Saturday morning, Mr. Garcia took his two sons to the Aikido Institute, where they are enrolled in the children's program, to see an Aikido demonstration. It was an excellent performance by the senior students and instructors.

As they were leaving the Dojo, Mr. Garcia told me the reason he took his sons to see the demo: "I wanted them to see where they are going."

Mr. Garcia wanted his sons to keep their eyes on the goals as they move along the Aikido path. I wished that all the students in the Dojo had that insight.

As I have stated several times during the Basic classes, a sure way to learn Aikido techniques well is to follow these three steps. First, have a clear mental picture of the correct forms; second, command your body (yes, give an order to your body) to duplicate that exact form; and third, repeat these two steps over and over.

When a public demo is done in the right spirit, the performance is impeccable, especially when dan-ranked students and instructors are involved. As far as participants are concerned, a demo serves the same purpose as a grading test. When people show their best it is a sight to behold and to learn from. This is an opportunity for other students to watch and reinforce those mental images of techniques that they want to learn.

Everyone in the Dojo should plan to see the next demo in January 1998.

Self-transformation

The steps outlined above for learning a technique are the same steps to achieve self-transformation:

I Wanted Them to See Where They Are Going

1. Have a clear image in your mind of what you want to be or accomplish.

2. Find a way to get there and make up your mind to follow it.

3. Continuously reinforce the goal-image and fine-tune the way.

Many people fail at the first step because they don't have a clue where they want to go.

> "Tell me please which way I ought to go?" asked Alice.
>
> "That depends on where you want to go," said the Cheshire Cat.
>
> "I do not care where," replied Alice.
>
> "Then it does not matter which way you go," said the Cat.
>
> Lewis Carroll, *Alice in Wonderland*

If the goal is not clear then the present action is not directed toward that goal and hence is a waste of energy. In other words, every act that is not aimed at a purpose is a waste. Even if the purpose is recreation or Zen meditation it must be clear otherwise the result of the act may not have the desired effect.

Sometimes it is easier to affirm the purpose in small increments rather than trying to ponder the ultimate. In our dojo, for example, after completing the purposeful act of signing up, all one needs to do is keep training for the next rank. The rank requirements are already spelled out clearly. All one needs to do is check those requirements periodically, find a good model to emulate and copy, copy, copy (that is, train, train, train). Therefore, in addition to getting a good workout, I recommend that all students come to the dojo to train for the next rank.

Studying Aikido

I have often mentioned in the Basic classes that one should "study" Aikido. To "study" is to apply one's mind purposefully to the acquisition of knowledge or understanding. With regard to Aikido, such purposeful activities include asking questions of oneself or of a *sempai*, taking notes of techniques shown in a class or seminar, visualizing techniques to remember them, reading Aikido books, charting techniques to see how they relate to each other, watching live or video performance of techniques by experts, researching O Sensei's biography and the origins of Aikido.

Such mental activities will clarify what one wants out of Aikido and reinforce one's goal in Aikido. As the target becomes clearer our chance to hit it increases. This is not how Aikido is practiced traditionally, especially in Japan. But it is natural for people in our Western culture to use the intellect in the pursuit of knowledge. We should lean on our environment, in the pursuit of personal goals.

One of the values that underlie our Dojo Code is: "Wholeness: learn through both the body and the mind". If you show the mind clearly where it is supposed to go, it will command the body to get there. In fact, a basic tenet of all oriental martial art is: the mind-intent (*yi*) directs the energy (*ki*) and the energy moves the body. Therefore, it is reasonable, even advisable, to do mental Aikido exercises, to supplement the physical training on the mat.

Going to Iwama

One of the experts whom we want to emulate is Saito Morihiro Sensei, who emulated O Sensei.

I Wanted Them to See Where They Are Going

The best way to learn from Saito Sensei is to be an apprentice to him at his dojo in Iwama, Japan. All of our senior instructors have had such a privilege.

Once you are *uchideshi* there, you can "study" Aikido to your heart's content. You can do two things that you cannot do anywhere else in the world. You get to see Saito Sensei and the *sempai* perform the correct techniques daily. If your stay is sufficiently long, you cannot help but absorb those techniques in your mind and body. They will form the basic mold for further progress in Aikido.

Secondly, you get to experience firsthand the environment in which Aikido was developed. This experience has the same effect on a serious student of Aikido as a visit to Paris or Rome has on a Renaissance art lover or a visit to the Napa Valley wineries on a wine connoisseur.

Aikido was created and transmitted in and through a cultural backdrop that is very different from western culture. It is important for the serious students to understand such fundamental concepts as *shuren* (arduous practice), *rei*

17

(propriety) and *giri* (obligation) etc. in order to get the most out of Aikido practice.

I am not suggesting that one should go to Iwama, adopt the traditions and techniques and transport them as-is back to the United States. On the contrary, one should understand the principles underlying those traditions and techniques then apply them in one's own environment back home in the most suitable form.

I feel that this is such an integral part of training for the advanced student that I have made a two-week apprenticeship in Iwama a requirement for fourth dan. Also, as an incentive, every class taken in Iwama counts as a full training day toward the next rank, in other words, since there are normally two classes a day in Iwama you get credit for two training days for each day there. So if anyone is serious about studying Aikido, go for it.

January 1, 1997

5

What Aikido Does to You

One time, during a discussion about the virtues of Aikido, my wife asked why certain people who have been practicing Aikido for decades are capable of doing bad things such as violating basic moral standards. This was a tough one; not because it is difficult to answer but because the answer is difficult to understand unless you have been practicing Aikido for a long time. I managed to explain it to her and thought that others may wonder about the same thing, so I am sharing it here.

What does the practice of Aikido do to me?

Simply put, Aikido transforms you into a human being who can live in harmony with its environment and who can focus on and accomplish any task efficiently. It will make you more efficient and more effective in what you do.

Of course, there are all these other secondary effects: increased physical and mental health, more meaning in daily life; increased self-confidence, etc ... Each one of these secondary effects is by itself a good-enough reason for anyone to commit to the practice of Aikido.

However, anyone who has trained for a long time or is looking forward to a lifetime of training cannot but wonder what deeper effect Aikido has had or will have on herself. Am I a better person now after twenty years of dedicated training? Why do I still react so strongly to such a simple gesture as a

AIKIDO INSIGHTS

flip by another driver on the road? Why do I still get so depressed when I cannot make ends meet?

Am I not supposed to ride above all these mundane worries and basic human emotions thanks to two decades of Aikido training?

After three decades of training, I can say that Aikido has not elevated me above the human condition. I still get angry, cry, feel sad and need money just like everyone else. But in a slightly different way.

I find that Aikido training affect people directly at the core of their being while leaving the outer layers almost untouched initially. It bypasses the social persona and get directly to the inner self.

The changes in the core will eventually and gradually effect changes in the outer layers. In other words, Aikido moves the whole of you (body, thoughts, emotions and feelings) to a different vantage point without changing your superficial make up. It does not make you more moral, smarter, kinder or more successful by societal standards. Aikido has not much to do with social values or religious virtues.

If you were a procrastinator before Aikido, you will still be a procrastinator after Aikido. If you were basically a liar you will still be a liar. If you were a drinker, you will still be a drinker. If you were a belligerent person, you will still be belligerent. If you believed in God, you will still believe in God. If you were an agnostic, you will still be an agnostic.

This is not to say that these characteristics of your basic self will not change. They will change, not as a direct effect of Aikido but as a result of change in your inner self caused by Aikido.

Aikido will convince you that the only way to live is in harmony with the universe and it trains you how to do that. During that training period, you will still retain your basic character.

However, after the core of your self has changed, the new self will realize that its current clothing is not compatible with its new internal make-up and decide to change it. Your new self will be able to make these secondary changes easily because Aikido has given you the tools: fluidity and focus.

Here is an example which may clarify this point further. After twenty years of doing Aikido, your self has changed so that it has become very efficient at managing its energy. It will find that most of the rules and conventions of the society that you live in are designed to minimize conflict among its members and therefore help to conserve its energy. Your self sees that these rules are compatible with its purpose and therefore decides to adopt them.

In this way you may decide to become more truthful. Not so much because you want to adopt a social virtue but because you know deeply that not respecting the truth leads to waste of energy. Or you become calmer, not because Aikido has brought you peace, but because you realize how costly emotions are in terms of energy. Or you may decide to cut down on the drinking, mainly because it robs you of precious energy.

Therefore, the secondary changes which may make you appear more virtuous or spiritual according to societal standards will be effected much later into Aiki training.

Thus one should not expect a person to become more virtuous or spiritual after doing Aikido for ten years. After, twenty years or thirty years, may be. And still, the visible transformation, if any, is only a secondary effect.

June 9, 1997

6

How Aikido Training Reduces Violence

Aikido is often dubbed the non-violent martial art. This phrase refers to the way one trains in Aikido. What most people do not realize is that Aikido training, besides being non-violent in nature, leads to reduced violence in our daily life. Here is how it works.

In one murder case, the victim was roller-skating in a deserted court. Two gang members walked by, one of them shouted obscene racial slurs, pulled a knife and stabbed the victim. Elsewhere, in a typical rape scenario, the victim walks home from the BART (train) station late in the evening, unaware that a man has been stalking her since she left the station. As she opens the door to her apartment, he forces himself in and assaults her. In another area of town, after a high school prom gala, a few friends drove home together. The passengers were teasing the driver who claimed that he was not drunk; he proceeded to demonstrate his sobriety by slamming on the gas pedal. He could not see the freeway exit sign timely and veered sharply at 100 mph to catch it. The car rolled over. Not too far from there, a frantic 911 call came from a child: his parents were arguing about lunch money for the kid then the father pushed the mother, she grabbed a kitchen knife, he tried to take it away but ended up with a severe cut to his face.

Murder. Rape. Car crash. Domestic fight. Violence exists when there is application of force of unexpected magnitude and timing, or simply put, extreme and sudden force.

In each of these cases of violence we note that the victims did not anticipate the timing of the force that came at them; therefore they could not blend with it and save themselves. If they had paid attention to certain detail, they would have been aware of the signs that led to the eventualities.

The roller-skater could have noticed that some strange-looking characters were approaching him and could have quickly changed direction since he was on skates.

The rape victim could have been aware of the darkness, the absence of people and even the silhouette lurking behind her; then she could have chosen a different path home.

The teenage driver was not aware that he was driving faster than he could control the car. If the windows were down, he would have noticed the engine and tire noise and the wind resistance and realized that the car was going very fast.

In the domestic violence case, the husband and wife should have been aware that they were both tired from the long day and that it was not a good time to talk about money issues.

The ability to be aware of the conditions and changes in oneself and the surrounding environment helps a person to anticipate certain eventualities and to prepare for them or avoid them altogether.

Attention to detail is an integral part of any true martial art practice and is especially a point of constant emphasis in our dojo. The strict etiquette and the insistence on the precision of the basic forms are intended to foster this care for detail. Awareness is part of our Dojo Code.

Therefore, such careless acts as bowing from the neck instead of from the waist and rushing through techniques so that one can go on to the next ones defeat the purpose of training in martial arts.

In the above described cases, if they were aware of the risk, the victims might have been able to blend with the aggressive force, instead of letting it overwhelm them.

"To blend" in this case means to reach out, connect and go with.

The roller-skater could, for instance, have begun to connect with the potential aggressors by greeting them "Hi! Howdy! Nice jacket". The greeting would not be expected by the aggressors and could have thrown them off a little. The skater could have used this opportunity to skate to a safe distance.

Similarly, if aware of the danger, the rape victim could at least project out her energy and create an aura of self-confidence while walking down the deserted street. This apparent self-assurance would make the potential rapist think twice before jumping on his prey.

If the teenager driver was well-trained in the art of blending, even when partially intoxicated, he would have instinctively responded to his friends' teasing in a less violent manner such as a verbal retort. Then he might have kept his calm and taken the freeway exit properly.

If they had practiced the art of blending, one of the fighting spouses could have stopped and listened to the other, understood his/her perspective and the fight could have been aborted.

In each of these cases there was a gap between the victim's perception of reality and the hard reality. The victim was not prepared to deal with the gap.

In Aikido, we constantly practice to close the gap between us and the attacker: We reach out, connect, re-align and blend smoothly with the aggressive energy.

For this blending practice to be useful in such potentially dangerous situations as described above, three conditions must be met: the attack must be realistic, the blending must be smooth and the practice should be internalized through several years of repetition.

During training, these three conditions are fulfilled as follows. A realistic attack is deliberate and carried out with focused energy. The smoothness of blending can be achieved only when techniques are slowed down and all the minute kinks are worked out meticulously. The internalization process takes place best when the exact same movement is repeated, not different versions each time.

Once this blending ability has become an integral part of oneself, that is, has become an instinct; it will automatically bridge any gap between us and reality. This bridge prevents a sudden and destructive meeting between us and reality, that is, violence. This is how the correct practice of Aikido can help to reduce violence.

Therefore, let's pay attention to detail in the dojo, work the fine points of the techniques in slow motion and concentrate on the basic forms.

September 8, 1997

AIKIDO INSIGHTS

7

A Perspective on Self-defense

Aikido is often referred to as a self-defense martial art. The term self-defense though, as used popularly, understates the depth of Aikido. In this essay I hope to rectify this situation.

Many people who drop in the Dojo to observe classes inquire about self-defense. Depending on how they address their questions I give them various answers. To most of these people, who are interested in defense against physical aggression I point them to other martial arts such as jujitsu, karate, tae kwon do, wing-chun, etc., and the model mugging classes offered by BAMM (Bay Area Model Mugging) on Sundays in our Dojo.

To some of these people who show a sincere interest specifically in Aikido I explain to them how Aikido helps them in self-defense. But I never had time to elaborate. This essay is an attempt to further elucidate the connection between Aikido and self-defense.

In the context of this discussion, self-defense is used as a synonym for self-preservation. I define self-defense as any attempt to preserve the self, with the term "self" used in its most comprehensive meaning. In this sense, any action (mental or physical) that is related to the preservation of the physical body, the energetic body, the mental body or the spiritual body is part of self-defense.

Thus, every one of the following situations constitutes an act of self-defense. You get out of an office building late at night and decide to wait for the company of co-workers to walk to the parking garage. During the flu season, you increase your daily intake of vitamin C to boost your immune system to protect against illness. At the end of a long workweek you instinctively seek seclusion to preserve what's left of your energy stock. In the middle of a life crisis, you decide to quit it all and take a vacation to preserve mental sanity. In daily life, you avoid the company of certain profane influences to preserve your spiritual health.

Self-preservation is an instinct of all living creatures. It makes a plant seek and move toward sunlight; it makes a small animal bite you when you get too close to it; it pumps up your adrenaline when you are frightened; it makes people resist change; it makes people avoid the unknown and shun other people who are different.

At the animal level, self-defense is strictly based on the instinct to preserve the physical part of the Self, that is, the physical body. This instinct can be cultivated to a very sophisticated level by training all parts of the Self. This training can be accomplished through a holistic martial art such as Aikido. To understand how this training takes place, we need to elaborate on the definition of Self-defense.

At a holistic level, Self-defense is any movement or tendency of the Self to minimize the effects of anything that tends to reduce its wholeness or impedes its natural growth. To defend itself against these adversarial elements in accordance with Aikido principles, the Self must use a three-part strategy.

In the first part, the Self must become aware of the adversarial elements. That is, it must know of the existence of the elements that threaten its wholeness and identify their potential effects. Here are some examples. To defend herself against cancer, a big-city dweller must be aware that she is living in a pollutant-filled environment, which may cause cancer if the necessary measures are not taken. A non-informed person may not know about this risk. To defend himself against possible self-annihilation through an automobile accident, a driver must be aware that wet pavement can cause collision. A driver under alcoholic influence may not be aware of such risk.

The possible threats to the Self are numerous, but there are certain types that are prevalent in certain locales and time periods. A few thousand years ago the common threat to mankind was probably wild animals. A few hundred years ago threats to the safety of human beings probably came from other human beings or diseases such as cholera and tuberculosis. Nowadays in industrialized nations, those threats are replaced by such things as risk of car accidents, cancer, heart attacks and AIDS.

Therefore, martial arts that were developed a hundred years ago by men to defend themselves against other men are no longer appropriate for self-defense in their original form and emphasis. The contemporary martial artist should know that the enemies are now different.

In our current environment, we should recognize that our most likely enemies are accidents, untamed virus and stress. The focus of our self-defense must change to address these threats. A highly skilled martial artist who dies from a stress-related disease cannot be regarded as being skilled in self-defense.

A person who is skilled in self-defense constantly evaluates the risk exposures that threaten his safety now and in the future. The sooner those risks are identified, the more effective the self-defense measure. The sooner a smoker understands the correlation between smoking and lung cancer, the better the chance for him to avoid this disease. The sooner a homeowner realizes the risks of living near rivers, on hillside, or near a fault line, the better the chance for her to defend her home against natural hazards. Awareness of the risks is the first step in self-defense.

In the second part of the self-defense strategy, the Self must acknowledge and learn about the adversarial elements. This does not mean waiting to find out the effects of an attack. Rather, it means that the Self should take the initiative to go forth to meet with the opposition and understand it. I observe that good surfers don't wait for the wave to hit them but they swim toward the wave and meet it; similarly skilled drivers begin lean on the steering wheel before the curve not at the exact time when the road curves around.

For example, you are involved in a disagreement with a teenager child. You can use your adult authority to settle the issue quickly, but that may not address the cause of the conflict. A better tactic may be to ask him about the reasons for his behavior and listen to his views. If his motives are plausible then acknowledge them and use them as a springboard to steer him toward the understanding that you would like him to attain.

Often, during this reconnaissance endeavor, when you understand the opponent's motives, his viewpoint and circumstances, the solution to the conflict becomes obvious. This initial study of the opponent is the essence of the first part of Sun-Tzu's famous phrase in his classic work, *Art of War*. "Know thy enemy, know thyself and the terrain and you will win a thousand battles".

After the surfer has met the wave and aligned himself with it, then the obvious way to go is to ride its momentum. Aligning oneself with the opposition may seem incomprehensible to most people but lies at the heart of Aikido self-defense.

In the third part of a holistic self-defense strategy, the Self must act to neutralize the adversarial elements. It must remove the reason for their existence or transform their nature into something more harmonious. As I mentioned earlier, when the Self has made the initial effort to align itself with the opposition, the way to restore harmony is obvious. For example, the cure for a disease is sometime obtained from using its causal elements. The principle of vaccination lies in inoculating the patient with the same virus that causes the disease with the expectation that it will stimulate the production of antibodies to fight off future viral attacks.

Similarly, the effective way to fight obesity is not to drastically curtail the food intake. Rather, the obese person should first study his own personality to understand the reasons for overeating. If stress is a causal factor, then take up yoga or similar practice. In the meantime, eat well and appreciate the food. Take time to taste, chew and savor. Then the food is better digested, nutrient absorption is more efficient and food consumption naturally decreases.

Firefighters use this strategy in fire suppression when they encircle the fire zone with a ring of fire that would eliminate the fuel load and isolate the main fire. Another technique would be to create an explosion that would suck out oxygen and deprive the fire of its main causative agent.

At the personal level, one of the most effective techniques for controlling internal outburst of energy such as desires or emotions is not to stifle them or ignore them but ride them then transmute them. Thus, stress and anger can often be managed by spending the energy in a workout that would be more beneficial to our health.

In summary, the three elements of self-defense that we learn and practice in Aikido are: be aware of the potential risks of conflict; connect, understand and align with the conflict agents; and defuse the conflict by addressing its deeper cause.

We practice this principle daily in the dojo. When executing a technique in class, we learn to quickly size up the situation and become aware of our training partner's size, timing, distance and weapons and the surrounding mat space. Next, we connect, align and blend with our training partner. Finally, we redirect his energy to the neutral ground or to a place where it can be dispersed without harm to anyone else. While all martial arts incorporate the element of awareness, the elements of connection, blending and neutralization are specific to Aikido and a handful of other martial arts.

March 2, 1998

8

What Makes Aikido Aikido

There were people of various martial art backgrounds who enrolled in the dojo and who allowed their past experience to affect their present Aikido training. This is a natural process but from a certain point, if it is not controlled, would add so much foreign elements to the Aikido training that it would create confusion among the trainees. Knowing when the line is crossed and when Aikido is no longer Aikido is a necessary skill for instructors. As this is an extremely difficult skill to learn I offered the following guidelines to our instructors.

Where do those kicking techniques come from? Is that part of traditional Aikido? Someone may wonder when watching a demonstration of Aikido from a different school. Are we practicing the original style of Aikido in our dojo? Someone else may wonder after pondering on the difference between her current teacher's style of Aikido and that of a visiting Japanese sensei.

Whether they are doing pure Aikido is a concern that naturally troubles the serious students of Aikido. In this essay I propose a technical definition of Aikido that may shed some light on the issue. The perspective presented herein is based on personal experience and is not meant to represent an authoritative statement on the nature or essence of Aikido.

The question is particularly troubling for students of lineage schools such as ours. Especially, students at the instructor level may struggle with this question: How much can I deviate from the teaching that I received from my teacher while still honoring the lineage?

If these students do not resolve this internal questioning they may be loath to wander off the beaten path. They will not explore beyond the forms that have been handed down and will become copycat teachers instead of allowing spontaneous expression of the art. In this way they will stifle their own growth.

In my experience, an Aikido technique must possess the following physical characteristics:

1. Three phases of the technique are discernible: first, the aikidoist connects with the attacker and receives the attack; second, the aikidoist re-aligns behind the attacker's energy, and third, the aikidoist uses this energy to lead the aggressor to a neutral ground.

2. The participants use *tenkan* during the re-alignment phase and use *irimi* -based motion for the initial connection and the throwing phase. In *irimi*, the arms, hips and legs are in triangular stance (*hanmi*) and focus toward the direction of the motion. In *tenkan*, the arms, hips and legs move in circles.

3. The motion for the technique originates from the feet (or part of the body in contact with the ground), then is enhanced by the hips and expressed through the arms. Alternatively it can originate from the hips, be grounded through the feet and be expressed through the arms.

4. The spine and the head are generally aligned.

5. Hands and arms generally move up and down in the front of the body.

6. During movement, joints are never locked, especially elbows, hips and knees.

7. At the advanced level, the techniques must be initiated before the manifestation of the attack.

8. Weapons work must follow the same principles as body techniques since they are considered as extensions of the limbs.

With few exceptions, a movement that does not exhibit all of the above characteristics is not an Aikido technique.

On a holistic level, it would be difficult to label something as Aikido if one of the following characteristics is absent:

1. Intent to restore and preserve overall balance: the persons doing Aikido must have, and exhibit, the intent to restore balance in a conflict situation. If there is any intent to separate, stand out, create conflict, destroy, maim or kill then there is no Aikido.

2. Integrity of movement: in performing Aikido movement, the performer must attempt to achieve an inner alignment of all body parts and move with the whole body as one unit. In Aikido techniques, this inner alignment is achieved through *hanmi* (triangular stance) when stationary,

and through *irimi* (moving forward using *hanmi*) or *tenkan* (moving circularly by turning the hips) when in motion. If one body part is left out in a movement, then the movement is not part of Aikido.

3. Harmonious interaction: in an Aikido practice the participants must interact with each other in a harmonious manner, alternating between *ukemi* (receiving) and *kokyuu* (extension). The energies should flow smoothly with no sudden interruption or burst. If one of the participants looses the connection with the other, there is a gap in the flow; if he does not receive when the other comes forward then there is a clash. If there are gaps or clashes during the interaction, then it is not Aikido.

The above discussion is aimed to benefit students at the instructor level (*sandan* and above) and pre-supposes proficiency in basic Aikido techniques. These students can begin to express themselves more freely using the above criteria. They should teach the Aikido that they understand and that comes forth naturally rather than repeat their teacher's teaching.

As for lineage materials, only those that are consistent with the above criteria need to be preserved; the rest constitutes personal expressions of the teachers in the lineage.

However, if a teacher's experiments take him significantly away from the defining criteria described above, his art has changed at the core and no longer represents Aikido. He may have created a wonderful new art but he should be cautious about labeling his art Aikido.

Other students not yet at the instructor level need not concern themselves with the detail of this discussion but should be aware that the term "Aikido" refers to a well-defined art. Like other arts, it has a set of basic techniques that forms its core and that every aspiring artist must learn. And like other arts, after the artist has internalized the basic forms, she must transcend them in order to grow.

From that point on, the art is expressed through the artist in a plenitude of colors. Then it is meaningless to look for the original art in such expressions; the art is in the artist. Similarly in the Aikido world, purity of styles is not a relevant concern for a student. What's important is how best to absorb the teaching of the current teacher. The best thing for a student to do is carry out exactly the teacher's instructions and search for their meaning in study and practice.

June 4, 1998

9

Writing About Aikido Is Part of Aikido Training

I started a newsletter at the Aikido Institute Oakland in the early 1990's and encouraged students to write articles for it. The article below explains how such writing is an integral part of the student's training.

The underlying values of the society that we live in are based on rationality. Concepts of fairness, efficiency and reasonableness are governing principles in all of our social structures. We are all conditioned to rational behavior and our whole social system including the education system supports such behavior. Therefore, it is natural for someone raised in this Western society to learn by thinking, asking questions and accepting what seems logical or rational as part of worthy knowledge.

In the spirit of Aikido, we should lean on this support system in the pursuit of knowledge, even knowledge as exotic as Aikido. We should raise questions, think about what makes sense and proceed with what makes the most sense in the practice of Aikido. In other words, we should involve the intellect in the study of Aikido. We should study it as we study any other formal sciences. We should verbalize our thoughts and organize them into comprehensive logical edifices. We should write papers and theses to explain this knowledge and its applications. In this way, we can share it with other people and at the same time test the validity of our understanding.

This mental activity will reinforce the knowledge accumulated by the body through physical training. For example, knowing the reason for executing a specific movement will help the Aikido student to see the logic behind the movement and accept it as a worthy goal for the body to strive for. By doing so, this student will have aligned body and mind behind the task of learning the move.

We should note that this logical approach to learning might not apply in other parts of the world where social behavior is governed by religious beliefs or social hierarchy and authority rather than individuality and rationality.

Rei – Proper conduct

In many parts of Asia for example, learning an art consists mainly of copying exactly what the teacher does for years and years without any questioning. This approach is natural in that part of the world and it works there because it is aligned with the local social system. A person raised in traditional Asia will readily accept any statement or instruction from the teacher as a worthwhile goal to strive for, irrespective of its logic. Such an approach would not work in America.

Aikido was created in such a traditional Asian milieu and was propagated through mechanisms which retain the ancillary social baggage. It is important for an Aikido teacher to discern what constitutes the social baggage and what constitutes Aikido. This teacher should then re-package Aikido using the current prevalent social concepts and make it part of mainstream education.

In summary, if education involves questioning, reading and writing then let's do some of these in learning Aikido.

June 4, 1998

10

Hard Training and Soft Training

A prospective student came by to watch an Aikido class and observed that there was no mention of Ki or energy practices. He was attracted to the concept of harmonizing with the Ki of the universe and wanted to know how our training embodies this concept. I gave him a short version of the following explanation.

Hard training, in the context of Aikido training, does not necessarily mean sweating it out on the mat. It is often the soft training that we need the most and that is hard to do.

For the purpose of this essay, hard and soft pertain to the method of training rather than the physical characteristics of techniques. A useful analogy is the distinction between hardware and software. The hard stuff refers to the tangible outer parts and the soft stuff refers to the non-visible inner parts.

Hard training then refers to the physical training involving martial art techniques. Soft training refers to the less tangible aspect of martial training that involves behavioral practices and *Ki* training.

Before we get into detailed discussion there is another distinction that will be helpful.

Martial arts can be generally categorized into external styles or internal styles, depending on the degree of emphasis on the physical body versus the internal energy. Generally speaking, the external styles use the hard method and the internal styles use the soft method.

External martial arts focus on the physical characteristics such as forms, muscular power and speed. They are often displayed as complex, fast and explosive movements. Internal arts put emphasis on what happens inside the body such as energy sensitivity, energy extension and mind-body connection. The external display of internal arts consists of simple and subtle motion sometimes performed at a slower pace. In this categorization of martial arts, Aikido is probably closer to the internal styles. In fact, Aikido would be just a dance if devoid of the internal emphasis.

Of the two methods of training in the martial arts, hard training and soft training, the latter is more compatible with the internal styles.

The hard method of training is aimed at improving certain qualities of the physical bodies, notably power and speed. This method uses physical props such as weights, dummies and heavy bags. It involves training to increase muscular strength, harden body parts used for striking, increase the precision of strikes or kicks, and improve fighting strategy. This training method is normally based on coercion and fear and is often reinforced by a rigid etiquette.

The soft method of training is often aimed at improving the inner self. This method involves breathing exercises, slow motion practices designed to bridge the external motion with the internal energy circulation, exercises aimed at gaining control of inner parts of the body, and meditative techniques. This method is not effective if imposed on the trainee by the instructor. It works only when the trainee is motivated by an intense desire to improve.

External martial arts, such as Okinawan karate and most Wushu styles, often use the hard training method. Internal martial arts such as Tai Chi Chuan often use the soft training method.

However, in a given martial art, the teacher can emphasize either the hard or the soft method, depending on his background, skill level and training goal.

Aikido is not regarded as a true internal style because it lacks a structure for internal energy work. O Sensei might have talked about *ki* and demonstrated the expression of *ki* but he did not leave a detailed method for harnessing or studying *ki*. Some of his early apprentices undertook the task of exploring the internal aspect of Aikido personally and designed their own systems. Koichi Tohei Sensei developed the *ki* principles taught in his organization; Mutsuro Nakazono Sensei devoted his time to *Kototama* study, Rinjiro Shirata Sensei blended Shinto purification exercises into his Aikido teaching.

The rest of us will have to find that internal component of Aikido ourselves. To get there, we need to use the soft training method.

AIKIDO INSIGHTS

My experience suggests that all martial art training should begin with hard training and gradually shift toward soft training. The timing and the extent of this shift depend on the type of martial art and the trainee.

For our Aikido training to be complete, this shift should take place soon after we have achieved a reasonable proficiency of forms. Various ways to do soft training in Aikido include: breathing exercises, concentrating on smoothness instead of power, visualizing techniques, learning patience from coaching new students, practicing *rei*, etc.

These seemingly non-technical practices form the core of soft training in Aikido and will facilitate the subsequent transition into spiritual practices.

In my view, our Aikido training should progress through these ten phases:

1. Strength: physical strength is built up.

2. Flexibility: limbs and hips become more flexible.

3. Coordination: all parts of the body are aligned in stance and motion.

4. Forms: forms become precise and a repertoire of basic techniques is mastered.

5. Timing: timing is mastered so that techniques do not appear fast but are always well timed.

6. Power: *kokyu* is mastered so that power is delivered effortlessly.

7. Energy: internal *ki* circulation is controlled at will.

8. Integration: *Takemusu Aiki* is achieved.

9. Mind practices: at this stage the training consists of practices to control the intent.

10. Spiritual practices: these are aimed at achieving an awareness of our fundamental connection with the universe.

This is how I see the Aikido journey. I have quite a distance to cover so I am not ready to recommend the exact same path to everyone. However, I urge all serious students of Aikido to search deep and clarify their own path so that their training can become purposeful and hence, more effective.

September 7, 1998

11

Prepaid Luck

I had instituted a dojo code that includes an obligation to share (I do my best, persevere and share in my practice) and often asked the students in the children program to give examples of how they applied the code. Some children could not connect sharing with Aikido training. I observed then that even adults did not take the sharing aspect seriously. So I wrote this article to point out the benefit of sharing.

Luck is defined as a chance happening of events that brings some advantage to us. It is something good that happens to us that does not seem to be the result of our action or is not normally expected.

Most of us believe in the concept of fairness that is inherent in the Golden Rule: do not do unto others what you do not want done unto you. We normally also subscribe to the corollaries: we get what we deserve; there is no free lunch; there is no gain without pain. In essence, there seems to exist in each of us a fundamental belief in a natural balance of good and evil in the world. Whether this belief is part of an inborn instinct or derives from a learned virtue is not the subject of this discussion.

In this essay I review the practical application of the Golden Rule: if I do a good turn to someone I can rightly expect something good coming my way in the future as a result of this good deed.

If I look after my neighbors' house while they are on vacation, then it would be normal for me to expect them to return the favor in future. It seems fair and logical for my neighbors to repay a debt. Taking this reasoning further, if I make the effort to help a stranger in needs then I believe that when trouble befalls me help will be forthcoming from someone, maybe another stranger. Most people would agree that this is a fair exchange. However, not many will believe in the materialization of the exchange since the logic is not so obvious: why would a stranger help me when he does not owe me anything? Here belief would have to be anchored in religious faith. One would have to believe that there is a divine force which ensures the fairness of all human transactions.

Carrying this line of thought a step further, if I always work hard, always lend a hand to people in needs and do the right things according to my conscience, can I expect to win the lottery when I suddenly need funds to bail me out of deep trouble? Why not? It would be just fair. But is there any logic to this? It is a long stretch for most of us to seriously consider the question. There seems to be no logical correlation between my moral and altruistic behavior and the good fortune of winning the lottery.

Now suppose I believe that the universe is one giant intelligent Being whose sole goal is to further its growth. This Being then would react favorably to anything that helps to promote its goal.

Suppose also that the growth of this Being is achieved through the growth of each and all of its components. Then, as one of the components of this Being, when I pursue my own growth I also contribute to the growth of this larger Being. Since I am doing a favor to it, it is fair and logical for me to expect this Being to help me in my personal endeavor.

Since this help comes from an entity as large and intelligent as the universe, it will occur under a set of circumstances that may be beyond my grasp. This means that help can come

Prepaid Luck

under any guise and at any time, even when I expect it the least.

So when I live my life correctly according to universal principles, that is, when I take good care of myself, of others and my environment, then I score points with this great Being who is keeping tab of all my deeds. Then at some point, it's payback time. The great Being knows that it needs to save me in time of needs because I contribute to its growth.

In other words, living a correct life is tantamount to investing in a divine bank account that allows me to withdraw interest in terms of appropriate divine help when I need it. This help may come at a time when most people would least expect it, and hence may be regarded as pure luck.

From this viewpoint, luck can be purchased in advance and deposited with the great Being. This luck can then be withdrawn any time, under any circumstances as long as the request is loud and clear and it benefits the great Being. If I do not expend it all in my lifetime, I may leave it to my heirs and descendants. In the same vein, I may start my life with a beginning balance of luck bequeathed to me by my ancestors.

This concept of prepaid luck is at the foundation of the concept of "Te" in the *Tao Te King* of Lao Tsu. "Te" has been translated as "virtue" in the common literature. Its meaning is derived from the belief that one should live a virtuous life, in relation to the Tao, and build up goodwill with the Tao. In our terminology, one should live in accordance with natural principles and build a good rapport with the universe.

This concept of prepaid luck or divine goodwill is incorporated in the element of "sharing" in our Dojo Code: "I do my best, persevere and share in my practice."

This part of the Dojo Code relates to the way we expend our energy. First we focus our energy on doing our best in our current situation; second, we use the remaining energy to persevere, that is, invest in achieving a future goal. Third, if we still have energy left, we should invest in the great Being through sharing, that is, through doing the right things for the benefit of others and our environment without expecting a specific return.

Investing through sharing is a concept that may not initially make sense to most people; but if you follow the discussion above, it does yield dividend. The return is beyond our control but it comes at the most propitious times.

I consider this type of investment the best.

December 7, 1998

12

The Power and Techniques of Focusing

It was January and I was engaged in a conversation with students about their New Year's resolutions. Several people were on track with their plans but others admitted that they have not taken the first step whereas some thought that such resolutions were futile effort. I told the two latter groups that they needed to come to class more often. Here is why.

During training we do "*kiai*" to focus our energy. This focusing of energy is an essential element of martial arts. I explain this important concept in this essay.

The Meaning of Focus

In general, to focus means to bring some form of energy into convergence at one point. In terms of daily life, focusing on a purpose means channeling our various activities toward accomplishing that purpose.

Our daily life abounds with examples of focused energy. We can see because light rays focus in a specific way inside our eyes. If these light rays are out of focus we do not see well. You can lift an object with your arm because you direct your energy into the motion of grabbing and lifting. Anything that interrupts your focus such as a startling noise may cause you to drop the object.

You can converse meaningfully with someone at a party full of people because you focus your attention on what your interlocutor says. If an old friend passes by and catches your attention, then you may lose your focus and the thread of the conversation.

If the focus is total, we see only what we focus on, we hear only what we focus on, we feel only what we focus on, we smell only what we focus on and we taste only what we focus on. It can be said that we live the life pattern that we focus on. I believe that what one focuses on determines one's destiny. If I keep focusing on not being able to do high falls, I will not be able to do high falls. If I keep indulging in being sick, I will be in ill health most of the time. If I keep focusing on failure, I will fail most of the times. If I keep working on my goal, I will get there.

All living creatures have been granted an innate ability to focus on the basic instinct of self-preservation. For example, the photosensitive cells of plants focus on light so that plants naturally turn toward light sources for survival. Birds fly in "V" formation to ensure that they do not lose the leader who is in charge of looking for food.

Human beings can elevate this focus toward more sophisticated goals if they so choose. If they do not then their lives are controlled solely by the automatic survival focus.

The Power of Focus

At the macrocosm level, in the beginning, there was a balanced void. There was nothing but pure energy. Then there was a differentiation that caused some energies to align in a particular order and the rest to align in another order. That was the beginning of the creation of the universe and also the beginning of focusing.

At the cosmic level, focusing means aligning energies in a particular order. Without alignment, there is no orderly movement and stable things cannot be created. At the earthly level, if the current order is disturbed, say, our planet stops rotating or begins to rotate at an erratic rate, life on earth would not exist. If water does not flow in a sustained direction then there are no rivers, no hydraulic energy, no irrigation, no inland life, etc.

At the biological level, can you imagine the impact on a living being when its circulatory system suddenly refuses to perform its clockwork process? Or what if any organ in the human body suddenly stops focusing on doing whatever it is supposed to do to maintain the body in good health?

In your daily life you probably know that if you intend to do something, you should plan for it and take the first step soon, otherwise you will never do it. Just think of that closet or that garage that you were "thinking" of cleaning. Thinking about it is the first effort in rallying your energy on the subject. Focusing does not take place unless you sustain this effort by coming back to this subject again and doing something about it.

Imagine a thousand infantry troops standing in a field. Suddenly someone not in sight yells out the command "Charge!" Heads will turn in all direction to look for a leader then bodies will move in random directions in an ensuing stampede. Now in a different field imagine a commander on horseback shouting out the same order and heading toward an enemy post. You can visualize all troops rallying around the commander and charging in one direction.

This metaphor applies to our body and our life. For example, if I do not command the trillion cells in my body to remain healthy, they will remain sitting ducks to invading armies of viruses. Generally, if I do not focus on specific goals during my lifetime, at the end of it, I will have only existed and not accomplished anything worthy of a human being.

My point is this: if there is no focusing there is chaos. Therefore, to make progress along the life that was given to us we must focus our energy; otherwise this energy reverts to the primitive chaotic state, by default.

This may sound like a farfetched statement. But just think of those great beings whose accomplishments you admire. Jesus Christ, the Buddha, Henry Ford, Mother Theresa, Michael Jordan, etc. Their biographies reveal an intense and sustained focus on their goals.

Techniques for Focusing

When you hold a colorful object in front of a newborn baby it seems like it cannot see the object.

It is because the baby has not yet learned to order the various stimuli into a coherent shape and color. The process of education that a human baby undergoes from birth is essentially an exercise in organizing the world into a particular order, a focusing process.

Based on my experience there are some simple techniques that can help a person focus better.

Set goals and plan for them. To focus you need a clear target. If wearing a black belt has been a fuzzy thought that keeps surfacing from the back of your mind, you should face that thought squarely and recognize it as a worthy goal. Then you should outline a series of realistic steps that will take you there. For example attend classes five times a week till the date of the next exam.

Your goal may be simply to learn high falls. In this case you should get a very precise picture of a high fall in your mind by watching the experts. This picture will be the goal that guides the movement and position of each part of your body as it takes off. The clearer the goal the sharper the focus.

A related technique to goal-setting is to decide on priority. Attribute a value to each goal. Or rank them in importance. You should know which of these activities is more important to you: have dinner with your spouse tonight, go and train at the dojo or put in some overtime in the office. If you do not consciously set the priority, the circumstances and your survival instinct will dictate your life.

Another technique is to enlist the help of other people and resources. Use an organizer or a planner. Tell people whom you trust about your goal, because they may help propel you into taking the first step of your plan or will remind you of your goal. Sign up for programs that monitor your progress, such as a weight reduction program or a tobacco cessation program. Set up things around you so that they remind you of your goals. One of our earlier *uchideshi* taped a picture of an open hand doing *kokyū* on his bedroom door to remind him to do just that in class.

Review your goals often. Question the validity of your routine activities. What is the point of commuting daily for two hours to this job in San Francisco? These activities may serve goals that were once valid but if these goals are now buried in the subconscious mind they are no longer the foci of the activities. Answering such questions will bring your goals into the conscious realm and help to re-validate them.

An effective strategy to help retain focus on a goal is to eliminate potential distractions. Once the goal is set, discard any activities that do not contribute to its achievement. This will keep your life simple so that your goal always stands out. This is the strategy adopted by serious spiritual seekers such as monks. Without leading their austere lifestyle, you can always adopt the simple lifestyle of an *uchideshi*.

Periodically consider taking time out to reassess your goals and focus. Don't just take a vacation. Spend a little time during your time-out to examine your life and determine whether it needs some fine-tuning.

To focus on small tasks is a good way to practice the focusing skill for larger tasks. Focus on just driving. Focus on making an omelet for brunch. Focus on just walking. Focus on just taking one step at a time. Focus on each breath.

When something distracts you from your focus do not fight it because you will get entangled in it and lose your focus. Just ignore it. For example, when a random thought comes to you while you are focusing on your breath during meditation, just acknowledge it and let it go. When you are trying to complete an important project, don't bother fighting off criticisms related to a different project.

One critical but difficult skill to acquire is to refrain from indulging. To indulge means to give free rein to the sensation or the mood of the moment, irrespective of where it may take you and whether it relates to your goal. Indulging means letting go of your focus. The easiest way to combat indulgence is to take an immediate action toward focusing as soon as the urge to indulge arises. But do it right away before the sensation or the mood takes control of you. When the alarm goes off in the morning, get up. When it's time to say good-bye, leave.

The act of focusing consumes energy, just like it would take a lot of work to re-route a river or to dam it. Energy is needed to hold all kinds of distractions at bay while your main stream of energy moves toward your goal. People who engage in serious focusing always go into seclusion to complete their task. Therefore, get in the habit of saving your energy for these serious endeavors. Don't slam the door if you can just close it softly. Don't stay up late if you don't have to. Skip the party unless it gets you closer to your goal.

Focusing in Aikido Training

Instant and total shift of focus is a hallmark of an expert martial artist. She can instantly move her total energy at will to support any move or strike. In some martial arts there is no need for competition to determine the better martial artist. All it takes is a simple demonstration of the ability to cause instant and total shift of energy.

We practice this same skill regularly in classes. For example, the *kiai* during *tai no henko* or other technique is for summoning our energy and focusing it on the move or posture at hand. The *hanmi* posture has the sole purpose of focusing our energy toward the tip of the triangle. The constant effort to stay connected with *uke* is an exercise to focus on a moving target. At the advanced level *happo giri*, the *randori* practice and the *jyuwaza* practice are exercises to shift focus totally and quickly from one target to another.

The Dojo's Mission, Motto and Code of Etiquette are also tools that help us to focus during our training. Conformance to the Code of Etiquette creates an environment free of distractions so that we can focus on training. The Motto describes the essential elements in our daily practice to help focus our long-term training. The Mission reminds us of our purpose in training.

March 9, 1999

13

On Kata Practice

I finished practicing my Wu Tai Chi form one day when a recurring thought came to mind: why don't we have Aikido kata that we can practice on our days off the mat? Hitherto I never had the time to follow through with this thought. This time I was sipping tea in my backyard and had time to let the thought germinate and grow into this essay.

Most martial arts contain kata that are used in regular training. A kata is a set of predetermined forms that contain the basic moves that constitute the technical repertoire of the art. The kata are meant to be repetitive drills for the students to internalize these core moves.

In mainstream Aikido there are no formal kata. In the Aikido that we practice in the dojo there are two katas: the *13 Jo Kata* and the *31 Jo Kata*. There are other styles of Aikido that include more kata in their curriculum.

What is a Kata?

A kata is a sequence of forms that are meant to be repeated many times, usually as solo practice, until mastery. A kata is often composed of core movements from which other techniques are derived. These movements are linked so that one flows smoothly into the next one. A kata is essentially a codification of the most fundamental elements of techniques in a format that is conducive to repetitive practice.

In a way, the manner in which we drill paired exercises involving an *uke* and a *nage* would make them kata, if the exact same pattern is repeated. However, when a partner is involved it is difficult to control the variability, so in general, kata are designed for solo practice.

The Purpose of Kata Practice

The initial purpose of kata practice is to internalize the forms. The ultimate purpose of practicing kata is to transcend the forms. Initially the student's energy is used to learn and master the forms. The performance of the kata provides a vessel in which the energy can be contained. As the form is being internalized, the student will gradually require less concentration and effort to perform it. Under the right conditions, the energy that is not used in maintaining the vessel will propel awareness to higher levels. Ultimately, kata is a way to elevate awareness.

How Kata Practice Affect Us

Repetition is the mother of all skills. Repetition of anything (good or bad) helps to internalize it. That is, the item being repeated is drilled deeper into our core (our subconscious) with each repetition. The deeper it goes the more it molds our mental and physical traits. After a certain point it becomes such an integral part of the self that its manifestation is a self-expression. In other words, the kata becomes the person.

On Kata Practice

How To Practice Kata

We do not necessarily excel in everything that we repeat during our daily life. How much better do you brush your teeth now compared to ten years ago? Do you consider yourself a walking expert after having walked this earth for thirty years? In these cases the two missing ingredients that are necessary for mastery, in addition to repetition are clarity of goal and energetic contents.

Clarity of Goal

Normally, when we use our legs to walk, we are mainly interested in getting from one point to another point without falling or bumping into things. This is a relatively easy goal for any average person. But now, suppose each time you walk you want to get from point A to point B while treading on the least space; for example you want to walk on a one-inch wide line from A to B. If you consistently apply your effort to maintaining your balance within a one-inch wide line every time you walk, you may be able to perform the feat of rope walking after a year of practice.

If you do not set a clear and specific goal each time you use your body, the body will naturally follow the path of least resistance and do just enough to get by. Therefore, for successful kata practice, the student must have a very clear mental image of the forms that are to be mastered. The more detail, the more precise the image and the more successful the replication.

Due to the emphasis on precision most kata are designed for solo practice. This set up eliminates the variability that is introduced by a partner.

Energetic Content

If the student has a precise mental image of the form and repeats it often, she will master it over time. She will become more efficient at performing the form and will use diminishing amount of energy. At 5th *kyu* it took you a lot of concentration to do *morotedori kokyuuho* correctly. Now at *nidan* this same technique requires hardly the same effort. Many people will be content with this state and think of it as proficiency. They will not apply much energy into executing the technique.

But if at *nidan* you devote the same amount of energy as you did at 5th *kyu* to perform *kokyuuho*, the excess energy not required by the form will carry your awareness to a higher level. For example, this energy will begin to make spontaneous energetic connections between *kokyuuho* and other techniques that use a similar energetic path. This is not just a mental connection but a connection that is effected by your total energy body. This is the time when one feels that something suddenly clicks. Previously disparate concepts or movements now become congruent.

The Risk of Kata Practice

The discussion above implies that if the martial artist is to transcend forms and get to the essence of the martial art, he must constantly practice kata with a precise mental image of the kata and with a beginner's intensity. Although beneficial, this type of practice carries the inherent risk that the kata becomes the ultimate training goal.

When a martial art is replete with kata the inevitable temptation is to make them the ultimate training goals. Our restless mind needs endless activity. It feeds on new and interesting things and thrives in diversity. After one has learned all the kata the training gets boring and one starts to look for new kata or new variations. The mind may even tell us that there is nothing else to be learned from our current teacher or current art. This is when students start to lose interest in regular training and look for new training partners, new teachers, new dojos or new arts.

It is my guess that O Sensei did not leave us kata for that reason. However, we should practice our techniques as if they are kata. We should have a precise picture of the techniques with all the detail in our mind; we should perform the techniques over and over without changing the detail; we should do each repetition with the same intensity as if it was our first time.

June 13, 1999

AIKIDO INSIGHTS

14

Service as Part of Aikido Training

At a ceremony to honor former uchideshi of the Oakland Dojo I touched on a key aspect of uchideshi training that is not generally known, namely, service. I explain here how this concept applies, in a larger sense, to our daily Aikido training.

We practice service daily in the Dojo. Some examples are: taking *ukemi*, bringing flowers for the *shomen*, helping a beginner, and sweeping the mat.

What Is Service?

The word "service" is derived from the word "slave" which has an unfortunate historical connotation. Nonetheless, devoted service, irrespective of who performs it, is what elevates an ordinary person to higher spiritual states.

From the perspective of a servant, an act of service consists of four elements: (1) a recipient of the service (a person, an idol or a cause), (2) an awareness of the needs of the recipient, (3) a willingness to give oneself to fulfill the needs of the recipient unquestioningly (4) a lack of expectation of any reward or return.

How Do We Practice Service on the Mat?

In the context of energy movement, when I serve another person, I extend my energetic radar toward that person and lock in so that I can detect the needs of that person and fulfill them. That is what lovers do in a date. That is what we do as *uke* when we train on the mat. We lock our energy onto our partner so that we can blend with her energy. In this way, we practice service when we maintain our energetic connection with our partner while receiving or executing techniques.

This connection should be unquestioning, that is, undisturbed by our questioning mind. During a technique, the moment we evaluate or let an emotion set in we stop being part of the flow and we lose the connection.

This connection should be unconditional. To truly serve your training partner, you should keep giving him 100% of your energy while engaged in the technique, even if he does not seem to appreciate your gift, even if he behaves with arrogance, or even if you don't like him as a person.

Therefore, if I am to serve my training partner, I should focus on his needs and limitations rather than just execute the technique according to my own needs. That is, I should adjust the speed, power and complexity of movement to my partner's level. My training partner's needs should take precedence over my egocentric tendency.

Practicing Service Off The Mat

There are several opportunities to practice service off the mat, such as supporting special events sponsored by the dojo, helping to organize dojo activities and helping in propagating Aikido.

Service as Part of Aikido Training

This spirit of service emanating from the membership is what differentiates a dojo from a business-oriented gymnasium.

We can extend this practice to our daily life. Here is a common example: a mother serves her family so well that at dinner time, as soon as her child looks up from his plate to scan the table, she has already grabbed his favorite salad dressing and put it in front of him. In the same way, we can practice attending to the needs of a person with whom we come in contact daily.

If your purpose in service is to learn, the recipient of your service does not have to merit it. You can serve your spouse, your parents, your children, your president, your sensei or your country even when they do not seem to deserve the service. Just use them as targets for practice. You don't have to wait for the room to get dirty to clean it. You don't have to wait for the *shomen* to get dusty before you wipe it. Your president does not have to be an honest person for you to take orders from him. Your sensei does not need to like you for you to help him with dojo tasks. Of course the more worthy the recipient the easier your practice is.

How Does Serving Others Help Me?

Although an expectation of reward negates the meaning of service, true service is rewarding in several ways.

The desire to serve stems from an inborn instinct to return to the source and get closer to our creator. The more we become aware of the fact that we all came from, and belong to, an eternal consciousness, the more we feel the need to serve all others which are parts of this larger consciousness. The reverse is also true. The more we practice serving others, the more we become aware that we are somehow linked at the most basic level to the others whom we serve. Therefore, practicing service satisfies an inborn human instinct and brings a sense of fulfillment that cannot be obtained in any other ways. Serving others strengthens the feeling that we are part of a larger being and increases our sense of security and self-confidence.

At a more pragmatic level, one who serves others well also acquires three important skills: a heightened sensitivity, the skill to connect easily with another human being and the skill to let go of personal prejudices in order to adapt.

These are the key skills for self-defense. The heightened sensitivity allows one to intuit an aggressor's move as soon as it is conceived, that is before it manifests. The connecting and adapting skills allow one to resolve the conflict in a harmonious way. These are the skills that *uchideshi* learn while serving their sensei and dojo.

September 14, 1999

15

Life is Conflict

In May 2000 I relocated from Oakland to Davis and gave a presentation to the nearby Woodland Rotary Club on Aikido and conflict resolution. While preparing for this presentation I recorded these thoughts.

Life is manifested through motion; motion needs effort; effort creates difference; difference results in conflict. Thus, life is full of conflict and the only way to avoid conflict totally is to be motionless, that is, not alive. Simplistic reasoning you might say, but I believe it summarizes a truth of life.

The "conflict" of life is simply the interplay of two basic phenomena: expansion of energy and contraction of energy. At the human scale, these two phenomena manifest as focusing activities and dissolving activities.

Focusing activities are those such as deciding, voting, clarifying, writing, planning, organizing, controlling, thinking, and moving voluntarily. They all require channeling our energy flow along a narrow path toward a pre-determined goal.

Dissolving activities are those such as relaxing, daydreaming, imagining, reading, watching, sleeping and moving involuntarily. They all involve a meltdown or expansion of our energy: we let loose and take in what energy comes our way.

AIKIDO INSIGHTS

An apparent conflict takes place when our consciousness is not fully engaged in one activity but straddles a focusing activity and a dissolving activity. For example, we feel "conflict" when we do something that we really do not want to: some part of our consciousness wants to focus on the action, and another part wants to let go of it. In another example, "conflict" happens when we engage in a fight with a brother: a part of us wants to focus on taking him down but a part of us wants to let go of the aggression and embrace him. If we were fighting against a sworn enemy with full intent to exterminate him, then there would be no conflict, at least from our vantage point.

Thus, most of the time, conflict is a personal perspective, devoid of moral content. It is strictly dependent on the vantage of our consciousness during the interplay of contraction and expansion of energy. The key to harmony lies in the proper positioning of our consciousness so that it is fully engaged in one single flow of energy at a time, either contracting or expanding.

We achieve this state by adopting a proper balance between focusing and dissolving. This is analogous to saying that we can achieve balance by proper balancing. It is a vicious circle that is the mystery of life.

We get there by being there. This is difficult for the intellect to comprehend but is something that our body can actually understand well when we practice Aikido.

During Aikido training our body has to continuously alternate between extending (focusing) and receiving (dissolving) energy in order to remain in harmony with our training partner. If we yield too much then we create a gap between us and our partner that will draw her in and she will run over us. If we extend too much then we will intrude into our partner's body and break it or hurt it in some manner. Every Aikido technique contains this dynamic adjustment.

With regular and long-term practice our body becomes skilled in achieving and maintaining a dynamic harmony with our surrounding, without our consciousness being aware of this state. That is, we may get there by being there without even knowing it.

During Aikido training we learn to neutralize the apparent conflict of life. We eventually come to the understanding that this perceived conflict is not something really bad after all: it is how life teaches us valuable lessons about living.

June 27, 2000

16

From Conflict to Harmony

As I was settling in the city of Davis, California, I wanted to share the concept of conflict resolution that is embedded in Aikido with my new community. I wrote this piece which was published in the Op-Ed section of the local daily newspaper, the Davis Enterprise.

During the early 1990s, at my former employer I had to implement certain cost-cutting measures that affected our work processes. One of my staff at the time (Let's call him Grump) rebelled against the changes, instigated insurgency among the rest of the staff then finally left for another job. I realized that I had failed in some respect as a manager.

However, some years later, to my surprise, Grump came to my farewell luncheon before I left for another job, shook my hands and in a sincere manner, thanked me for my patience and for the professional knowledge that I have imparted to him. I must have done something right. With hindsight I offer below an analysis of how I handled this conflict, pointing out the successful strategies and those that did not work so well.

Let me begin with a simple definition of conflict and outline in simple terms a strategy that I believe is the best for resolving interpersonal conflict. For our purpose, we will say that harmony exists when people's energies blend together and flow freely. There is conflict between two persons when the confluence of their energies creates a temporary stagnation.

Let's take on the role of one of the persons and call the other "opponent" and label his energy "aggressive". One way to relieve the stagnation and restore harmonious flow is the following four-step strategy:

1. Connect with the opponent.

2. Receive the aggressive energy.

3. Align with the aggressive energy.

4. Direct the aggressive energy to neutral ground.

Simple and logical concept you might say, but in my experience its successful application requires engagement of our total being, that is, body, heart and mind. Let me go through these four steps in reference to the Grump case.

Connect

For our purpose, "connect" means reach out and be in touch with the core of the would-be opponent. This technique requires a pro-active attitude and an alert mental state. I failed here. In my daily contact with staff I was not aware of subtle changes in Grump's behavior, which were warning signs of the brewing rebellion. I talked to Grump daily but I was talking to the superficial person. I did not connect sufficiently with his deeper self to be aware that his energy had been hitting the apparent walls that I set up when I re-organized the department. I should have been more in touch with the real persons in my staff.

"Connect with the opponent" requires us to constantly project our energy sensors out and constantly be aware of the changes in our surroundings. This technique requires us to be ready to initiate the first move. Even for purpose of defense; we should control the situation at the outset, rather than let the situation cause us to react.

The lesson I learned here was that I should be constantly aware of the changes in people around me. With a sustained daily effort to connect with people one gradually gets in the habit of including other people as if they and we are in the same family. This automatic "inclusion" of the other person helps to pre-empt a potential conflict.

Receive

At this stage of the conflict the opponent's energy has gathered sufficient momentum to manifest as an aggressive force. "Receive" means to allow this force to penetrate our defense to the extent that is sufficient for us to size it up and understand it. The premise is that if we do not understand the "enemy" we cannot deal with it effectively.

I did this with Grump. I invited him into my office several times and listened to him as he related his tribulations. I listened intently, and sincerely tried to understand the reason for his unhappiness. Looking back, I think it was this empathy from my part that Grump appreciated the most and that made him come to my farewell party.

In our daily life, perhaps because of fear or insecurity, we often put up our defense wall too soon or set up too many layers of defense before we have the chance to understand what is coming at us.

"Receive" means to be open and exposed but does not mean that we should open all the doors and invite the enemy in to our deepest core. We should receive while staying connected (per step one). That is, we yield in a controlled manner, while keeping the aggressive force in check. I allowed Grump to express his dissatisfaction but in a controlled environment and while I was following his mental move closely. I was "with" him the whole time.

Applying this technique requires that we resist the urge of fight or flight. In the face of aggression we should instead face it and receive it without being vulnerable.

Align

Herein lies the art of conflict resolution. As we receive the aggressive energy we move to get out of its path and re-align ourselves behind it. This is the most difficult of the four steps outlined above and takes years of practice to perfect.

I did this with Grump. I truly wanted to understand why he felt the way he did so I stepped into his shoes and tried to see eye to eye with him. When he ranted on with his complaints and accusations I listened but did not take them to heart; I did not stay on the path of the aggressive energy and let it crush me. I paused after his key statements and reran them in my mind to grasp his viewpoint. I also re-read all the pertinent memoranda that I sent to staff and other policy and procedure instructions, imagining how I would have felt as a staff person.

I even went to Grump's office and sat at his chair behind his desk, checked the ergonomics, etc. to see if I could detect any culprit of my employee's dissatisfaction. I chatted with his wife who was working in a different unit to see if I could detect any sign of conjugal distress. As a result, I gathered information that indicated that Grump had been preparing himself for a change in career. This desire to change and the accompanying stress had re-channeled his energy in a new direction that was at odd with the environment that I was trying to create in the office.

Grump's new energy could not flow freely when it met my energy that was reflected in the way I ran the department. But after I aligned my viewpoint with his perspective, I understood the nature of the aggression and its underlying cause. Once I understood this, I felt that the conflict was almost resolved.

Redirect

At this stage we are already aligned with the aggressive energy. Now we can take it into a new direction that would benefit both us and the aggressor - to a neutral ground. The way I did this with Grump was to chat with him about his long-term plan and help him identify the pros and cons of the various options. He wanted a career move but could not decide to leave the current employer. However, there was no room for his advancement here, and he hesitated to take a job with a new organization. Once I could see his preferred option I encouraged him to take the jump. He decided and left the organization. His energy flowed freely again. The conflict was resolved.

Note this difference. If Grump had resigned in anger to take up the new job, the end result would appear the same as above, but the conflict would not have been "resolved".

In conclusion, although I did not follow entirely the four-step strategy, I managed to restore harmony between Grump and I. I actually developed this strategy post facto by reviewing the detail of this incident and applied it retrospectively to validate it. I have seen this work in several other occasions with other people and in my personal life. The strategy works best when the four elements have been well assimilated and their application has become second nature. Although this assimilation takes years of deliberate practice, anyone can benefit from the strategy by consciously applying it. The initial effort might be arduous, but the peace and harmony that can be achieved is worth all of it.

February 26, 2001

17

Saito Sensei's Legacy

My late Aikido teacher, Morihiro Saito Shihan passed away on May 13, 2002, after a long and productive teaching career that took him all over the globe and brought the world to Iwama, Japan. I wrote this in memoriam piece to record his legacy.

Many of the greatest artists of all times devote all of their energy to the pursuit of excellence. That is how they became great and why they stood out from the crowd. Most of them would not accept students because these are impediments to their personal growth. However, there are a small number of great artists who save some of their energy, at the detriment of their own development, to reach back and help the rest of us move forward. Not unlike the bodhisattvas in the Buddhist tradition who postpone their own enlightenment in order to save the mass. Saito Sensei's life reflects this latter ideal.

Were it not for Saito Sensei's effort in distilling the Aikido techniques that he learned from O Sensei into basic and advanced categories and had he not care to emphasize the practice of basic techniques, then perhaps Aikido would not have enjoyed the solid hold that it now has in many parts of the world.

Saito Sensei has not just shown the world the beauty of the art that he has mastered, he has shown and taught many people the way to teach and share this art with the world. In this sense, he was not just a great artist; he was a great teacher who left a valuable legacy: the way to teach Aikido to all.

Therefore, to pay true homage to this great man, it is not enough for those who follow his footpath to practice Aikido and become strong warriors of peace. We should learn to be great teachers of Aikido and help propagate these teaching techniques.

In my view, the valuable teaching techniques that Saito Sensei left for us can be summarized as follows:

1. Understand the art thoroughly from *Kihon* to *Takemusu Aiki*.

2. Teach Aikido using a gradual method going from basic to advanced.

3. Constantly emphasize the practice of basic techniques.

Understand Kihon and Takemusu Aiki

Aikido techniques are not rigidly cast forms but rather dynamic principles in motion. The forms of a technique change according to the situation. A variety of forms can represent the same technique as long as certain principles that are the hallmark of the technique are preserved. A good Aikido teacher should be able to identify the core form of a technique and understand it so thoroughly that she can move fluidly between the core form and the multitude of variations of this core. This understanding should be internalized and not just intellectualized. The only way to reach this level is to persevere in the repetition of the core form.

Saito Sensei has established clearly the core form (*kihon waza*) of each key technique. This core form is defined not so much as an unchanging physical form, but as a set of relationships among body parts, a particular mental image and a particular set of "feelings". Those who have studied with Saito Sensei for a long time will remember these mental images and "feelings" (*kimochi*) associated with each of the key techniques. The core form is manifested differently under different circumstances. For example, different teachers will present the same core form differently under the same conditions, due mainly to their different physical, mental and emotional make-ups and states at that time and place.

Teach Aikido in a Methodical Manner

Certain Aikido teachers teach by simply expressing their own Aikido, that is, by demonstrating their techniques as they feel. These may be the ultimate physical expression of the art, but only a select few will be able to appreciate them, not the mass of beginners who are trying to learn Aikido.

The skilful teacher reaches out to the students at their level and entices them to progress by showing them the steps to the next level. In addition, the skilful teacher helps the students build a solid base by requiring constant practice of basic forms (simple versions of the core forms). The teacher then guides each student step by step all the way to *Takemusu Aiki*, the ultimate level.

This way of teaching requires the teacher to refrain from just a display of self and to focus on the students' needs instead, a most difficult requirement, but one that Saito Sensei always embodied. One just has to remember how Sensei explains a technique either at a seminar or in his books.

Constantly Emphasize Basic Techniques

Applying a methodical approach as described above is not enough. Emphasis on basic techniques means that students of all levels should spend more time and effort on basic techniques. This means that even advanced students and teachers should spend more effort on drilling the basics, through either personal training or teaching others.

Saito Sensei and the author,
Iwama, Japan, 1991

The ultimate expression of Aikido, *Takemusu Aiki*, cannot and should not be practiced. It is a natural result of all the practices leading up to it. A "practice" is a deliberate repetition. *Takemusu Aiki* cannot be deliberate, it is natural. Besides, if one "practices" *Takemusu Aiki* in the dojo, one may enjoy it but hardly any benefit will accrue to others.

Saito Sensei always included ample time in his classes for basic techniques. Aikido is built from the core out, or from the bottom up. We discover *Takemusu Aiki* by practicing more *irimi-nage* in basic form, not by doing more variations of this technique.

Thus, in my view, is the legacy of this great being, who not only showed us the Aiki path, but also taught us how to show this path to the rest of the world. He has done his work; what we are going to do with his legacy is up to us.

June 9, 2002

AIKIDO INSIGHTS

18

The Art of Peace

War sentiment was in the air when I wrote this piece. The Second Gulf War began a few months later amidst intense controversy about the reason for its prosecution. Within the U.S. the peace activists were waging war against the pro-war government. In the midst of this intense national debate I wanted to draw some attention to what peace really meant. I wrote this piece which was published in the Op-Ed section of the local newspaper, the Davis Enterprise.

Given the current state of tension in world affairs, there is an on-going popular debate on whether and how this country should wage war or create peace. There has been much discussion about the subject of war and peace in both world and national contexts, but often devoid of the linkage to the average human being.

In both pro and anti war camps, there are organizations that we can join, petitions that we can sign, and demonstrations that we can participate in. But is there something the average non-activist person can do on a daily basis? This article attempts to fill this void by offering a method for any individual to participate in the creation of peace. After all, we wage war only because we want to achieve peace.

We are not referring to the peace at the international level, but rather peace at the interpersonal level that affects us in our daily life. I believe that if people have peaceful relations with each other daily, the aggregate effect will generate true peace at the international level. Accordingly, irrespective of any political resolution to the conflict in the Middle East, if Israeli and Palestinian persons cannot relate peacefully with each other, the politically-achieved peace will be short-lived.

In this essay I draw on ancient wisdom that is brought forward to modern society by the art of Aikido and present a method to promote peaceful human relations. The word "Aikido" can be translated as "The Way to Harmonize with the Universe". It is a martial art rooted in old Japanese fighting arts, which is now often referred to as the "Art of Peace". It was created by a warrior well-versed in these fighting arts who sought and found spiritual enlightenment. The Founder created "Aikido as a means to reconcile the world" (in his own words).

For the sake of this essay, we introduce a definition of peace together with certain essential premises that may require a temporary leap of faith from the readers.

In the context of the universe as a vast field of energy, we define peace as a state of harmony in which energies flow without obstruction. To get a glimpse of this state, one can conjure up the image of a cascading mountain stream which flows through forests and valleys all the way to the ocean without being dammed along its course. This definition of peace reflects the dynamic interaction of energies in life and is akin to the harmony promoted by the art of *Feng-shui*. We shall use the terms "peace' and "harmony' interchangeably from here on.

Let's accept for the moment that there exists a super intelligence that oversees the multitudinous interactions of energies in the universe. Its purpose is to ensure that these energies flow harmonious in accordance with a set of immovable rules that we will refer to as Cosmic Law. According to this definition, adherence to Cosmic Law will bring Peace. A subset of this Cosmic Law states that peace is created and maintained by continuous flow. We will refer to this as the Law of Harmony.

We will presume that peace is the primordial state of this universe and that hindrances to peace can only be caused by semi-intelligent creatures that have the abilities to interfere with the Law of Harmony. One such type of creature is the human being. Due to their gregarious nature, human beings often act in groups such as congregations, societies and nations. Within each such group the qualities of individuals coalesce into the quality of the group. The way to truly change the quality of a group is to drill down to the individual and change the quality of each individual in the group. Thus, true peace is built one individual at a time.

As a corollary of the above definition of peace and the above-stated premises, true peace can only be achieved when each human being acts in tune with the Law of Harmony. This attunement must be pervasive, that is, must be present in transactions within oneself, with other human beings or with other elements of this universe. The rest of this essay describes the practical steps to generate harmony during the interchange among human beings.

During a human interchange, peace is threatened when energies generated by the inter-acting individuals collide and obstruct each other's paths. This obstruction interrupts the free flow of energies and creates an impasse, which can be viewed as a conflict. If this blockage is not removed timely, the dammed energies build up and resolve the blockage through a violent outburst. This is how conflict gives rise to violence.

Therefore, the key action in creating peace in human interaction is to keep the flow of energies from being interrupted. This can be done through a four-step strategy that is inherent in Aikido, the Art of Peace: reach out; receive; realign; and redirect. Each step in itself contributes to freeing energy blockage, but the four steps executed sequentially have a synergistic result.

The first step is to reach out. This step requires one to be in a constant state of awareness, to adopt a positive mental state at all times and to always take the initiative. In martial art parlance, this translates into the phrase "the best self-defense is often a pre-emptive strike". In a confrontation, the Aikido adept often makes the first move and sets the stage for all that follows.

In terms of daily life, to reach out is to take charge of one's life. It means planning for everything that we want to see happening in our life. Aikido is grounded in the belief that the mind controls the body and a thought generates a corresponding action; thus, anything that one visualizes and earnestly works for will actualize. We should avoid being in a reactive mode and wait for life events to force us into action. This pro-active attitude to life will help us identify and prevent any potential energy blockage. Even upon encountering a blockage this positive attitude helps one to immediately find an outlet that will restore the flow.

The practice of defensive driving is an example of this strategy. Always observe around and be aware of other drivers'

intent and take pre-emptive steps accordingly; do not wait for the need to react to another driver's abnormal maneuver.

The second step is to receive. The gist of this step consists of remaining open to receive an unknown oncoming source of energy until one has fully grasped what one is dealing with. To accomplish this we must consciously let our automatic defense system down momentarily, recognize and evaluate what is happening to us before responding. This is easier said than done since it requires a conscious effort to restrain our self-preservation instinct, which may trigger an automatic response. Thus, we should refrain from any negative or defensive behavior until we understand the nature of the aggression. The trick here is to remain open while simultaneously keeping the aggression in check so as not to compromise our core.

Receiving rather than blocking allows a continuous energy flow and promotes harmony. In our daily activities, the art of listening is an example of receiving. For example, upon being verbally attacked, one should pause, take stock, listen to the aggressor and try to understand his viewpoint instead of immediately retorting with invectives.

In the martial art context, rather than blocking an oncoming strike, the Aikido adept would give in in a controlled manner to receive the attack without exposing vulnerable spots while assessing the nature and intensity of the attack.

The third step is to re-align. This is by far the most difficult among the four steps. It requires a person to change his vantage point and see eye-to-eye and heart-to-heart with the other persons engaged in the exchange. This same principle is often used, albeit superficially, in undercover warfare and insurgency tactics, as well as in marketing strategies.

The ultimate goal may be to take over the control from within, but the change in perspective must be sincere and total. One has to let go of one's position and adopt the opposite position temporarily but wholeheartedly. This is a very conscious effort that takes a lot of patience and large amount of energy. It requires a total abandon of our perspective and a total immersion into a new perspective. This act removes any blockage to the oncoming energy and gives it free flow, thus fostering harmony.

Imagine starting a new job mid-career. The best way to be in harmony with your new workplace is to let go of all preconceived ideas about how certain things get done and to totally espouse the culture and style of the new environment.

In the context of Aikido, instead of attempting to immobilize or knock down the attacker, the adept executes a circular move and physically re-aligns her body side by side with the attacker or right behind his center, from where she can redirect him.

The fourth step is to redirect. After we have re-aligned with the adversary and understood where he is heading, we then take over the control from a centered position and lead him to a safe and neutral place where his energy can be dissipated or absorbed on neutral ground. This step comes naturally after re-alignment takes place, because when adversaries see eye to eye, they stand on the same side and become partners. In redirecting, we lead our new partner to a mutually beneficial perspective. This step should be done in the spirit of protecting our partner.

As an example, look at how early humans befriended and tamed fire to redirect this awesome source of energy to serve their needs.

In Aikido context, the adept leads her training partner to pin him safely on the ground or execute a throw to redirect him to another safe place that would not cause him harm.

How we redirect our partner depends on our spiritual make-up. A spiritually advanced person realizes that all beings are interconnected and understands that helping another person to resolve his energy blockage is the same as helping oneself. I remember reading in the news a while ago about the story of a priest who was robbed in the street at gunpoint and who eventually offered food and shelter to the robber. The robber later redeemed himself in society and wrote a letter to thank the priest for changing his life.

In the art of Aikido, the four steps described above, reaching out, receiving, realigning, and redirecting, are inherent in each technique. The student of Aikido practices them over and over with a training partner. This deliberate repetition of precise movements causes a psychosomatic transformation of the student such that this four-step strategy becomes ingrained into her personality.

People who do not study Aikido can use this strategy in their daily life, with more conscious effort. This strategy for promoting harmony can be summed in this formula: create flow and make all transitions smooth.

Any average person can practice and promote peace by gradually removing excessive contrast in daily activities: reduce sudden movements, curtail radical thoughts, use moderation in speech and behavior, refrain from extreme emotions, etc. as well as always looking for the positive. With practice, one will reach a state in which one can adapt to any set of circumstances while retaining one's integrity.

For those of us who are accustomed to being entertained by rapid change and a great variety of extreme stimuli this practice reduces the fun and thrills of life. Indeed, the cost of achieving peace includes foregoing much of what some may regard as an exciting life. The benefits, though, are a deeply rewarding sense of connection with all beings around us and the comfort of knowing that we are truly larger that our individual selves. The choice is yours.

October 2, 2002

19

Things Get Worse Before They Get Better

Saito Sensei passed away a couple of years ago and our Aikido world experienced the natural shake up that follows the death of a great leader. There was no bad blood, but it was sad to witness the fragmentation that took place within what was formerly a very homogeneous group of Aikido practitioners. I was ruminating on this state of affairs as I was driving home one day. Suddenly a car coming the other way cut in front of me to turn into a driveway. I saw it coming but it was veering in the opposite direction so I did not slow down. Apparently the other driver was attempting to align the car with the driveway by first veering right before turning left into the narrow driveway. I slammed on the brakes on time and avoided an accident. I later had this realization.

An ailment gets worse before healing.

All things quiet down before the storm.

To go forward you gather momentum by going back.

The car driver veers right to get ready to turn left.

To jump up you squat down first.

You wind back to swing the golf club forward.

Inhalation precedes coughing.

You raised you arm to strike down.

Therefore, when the opponent retreats watch out for his forward charge

When the opponent is inactive he may be preparing for action.

Before an event changes course it normally gathers momentum in the opposite direction

This is because energy must be built up and aligned in the new direction.

In a self-defense context,

One should remain in tune with the adversary's energy

And be ready to seize the opportunity.

Then one can stop the opponent's arm on the way up before it strikes down

One can thwart the attack as it is being conceived.

In life, when things are good one should know that bad times are nearby and prepare

When things hit bottom one should be ready for the rebound.

So they say: there is an opportunity in every crisis

The seed of the opposite is always present

This is the meaning of Tai Chi.

July 27, 2004

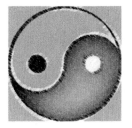

20

Dojo Expansion and Dojo Spirit

I opened a new dojo in Davis, California in December 2002. The student base grew so quickly that two years later we decided to double the mat space. On this occasion, just like in all prior instances that I have witnessed, the students contributed enormously to the work and strengthened the existing esprit de corps. This is what distinguishes a dojo from a fitness center or sports club. I pointed this out to the students.

Last month we doubled the mat area in the Dojo and added a multi-purpose room, a shower stall and an attic. Now students can enjoy safer training, especially during *bukiwaza* (weapons practice) classes, and adequate facility for the occasional party.

A contractor did most of the structural work but students undertook several tasks to prepare for the construction and to put the finishing touch. Most notably, students helped lay down the wood flooring for the mat and dealt successfully with the challenge of packing the tatami-size mats into the frame. Other tasks included padding and covering the post in the middle of the mat, hemming the carpet and painting the ceiling beam and the posts.

Almost all students chipped in to help. Several gave generously of their time. A student skilled in carpentry helped to coordinate all other students' work and took on tasks of his own such as painting the walls and building the attic.

As pointed out above, this expansion resulted in practical benefits to students. More space meant a bigger dojo. But the dojo also grew bigger in a different sense.

The spirit of the dojo expanded. When people came to help out with tasks after classes or with weekend projects they gave freely of their time and energy, that is, without expectation of returns, or simply without any expectation. Everyone enjoyed the work just for the sake of the work. Each sweep of the broom, each lifting of a tatami mat, each thread of the needle, each stroke of the paint brush, each pounding of the sledgehammer to align the mat was done as a gift of energy to the dojo. There was a certain joy in the air that blended everyone's energy together. That was the joyful spirit that begged to be expressed and that prompted me to lead the impromptu class after the last mat was put down. When people come together and put out this kind of disinterested energy, the energy is pure and serves as a medium that connects harmoniously all people involved.

This interpersonal connection exists only when energy is spent as a gift to the spirit, without any expectation as to the outcome. Everyone did their best in painting, sewing, cleaning, pounding on wood, adjusting mats, but no one was concerned about being perfect. This is a glimpse of the state of no-mind (*mushin*) that we aspire to in martial arts training. This is the state of mind that one needs to have when doing advanced training such as *jiyu-waza* (free-style techniques). During such training, our energy must be concentrated on the technique at hand. If the mind interferes by causing an expectation as to the outcome of a technique, one's energy becomes impure, and even for a fraction of a second, one loses the connection with the *uke* and the next techniques fail.

We should remember this in daily Aikido practice. When it is time to come to class, we just go to class and put out our best. We use the rank requirements to focus our training energy, without expecting reward or recognition of any kind. We give this training energy to the spirit, so whether or not we make progress does not matter, whether or not the sensei notices our effort does not matter, whether or not we rise in rank does not matter.

Any time one does any work with such a disinterested focus one is training toward the state of *mushin*. Beside training on the mat, opportunities for such work include sweeping the mat and cleaning the dojo after class.

Thus, we added space to the Dojo, but more importantly, we added to the dojo spirit.

November 7, 2004

21

Fitness, Aikido and Tai Chi

My wife's New Year's resolution was to do the Wu Tai Chi long form daily. She was wondering whether the slow movement of Tai Chi was enough exercise to maintain fitness. These are my views on fitness that I shared with her and now with you.

Does Aikido or Tai Chi help me get in good shape? This is probably the question that arises in many minds that are trying to decide on whether to sign up for one of these activities. The short answer is yes, improved fitness is one of the incidental benefits of training in Aikido or Tai Chi, but it takes a while to realize it.

Let's first define fitness. Fitness is generally viewed as more than general health. A physically fit person is already generally healthy and leads a more active life than one who is healthy but not fit. For the purpose of this discussion I suggest that physical fitness be measured in four dimensions: general health, endurance, flexibility, and healthy physique.

We will say that a person is physically fit if he or she possesses above average measures in these dimensions. An activity that results in an improvement in any one of these indicators improves physical fitness. Let's examine how Aikido and Tai Chi affect each of these dimensions of fitness.

General Health

Our immune system is the self-defense system of the body and protects our overall physical health. It helps the body combat most pathogenic agents and recover quickly from injury. The core of the immune system lies in the lymphatic system that includes the lymph, ducts and the lymph nodes. The primary function of this system is to evacuate toxins. If this system is weakened, the body is vulnerable and may succumb to disease-carrying agents.

The lymphatic system does not have a pump like the vascular system and is effective only when the lymph is circulated by muscular contraction, that is, body motion. Herein lies the benefit of exercises, especially those that activate lymph circulation. The correct practice Aikido and Tai Chi involves motion that continuously squeezes and relaxes the joints, where most lymph nodes are located. Such motion includes twisting of hips, stretching of neck, arm and leg joints. This type of motion acts as a pump for the lymph and helps in the elimination of toxins. This is how Aikido and Tai Chi contribute to the general health of a person.

Endurance

Breath control is key to endurance. When a person is out of breath too soon, he does not have endurance. Endurance is usually built up from constant repetition of the same physical exercises, whether aerobic or anaerobic. The body learns to become more efficient and consumes decreasing amounts of energy and hence less oxygen. In this way it endures, that is, builds the capacity to last longer. Aikido and Tai Chi practices are based on constant repetition of a vast array of movements. These practices build up endurance.

In addition, another factor that contributes to endurance is the mental control that is inherent in these two arts. This control is derived from the exercise of focused intent to move energy and the body, and allows the latter to transcend physical fatigue. Through constant practice of this mind-over-body control a person who perseveres in Aikido and Tai Chi will develop an above-average ability to endure.

Flexibility

A key training goal in Aikido and Tai Chi is to receive and blend with aggression. To accomplish this goal our body must be able to receive the oncoming energy in whatever shape or intensity. One way to do this is to be sufficiently supple to accommodate the variety of energy forms that come at us. By design, Aikido and Tai Chi techniques involve constant joint twisting and stretching that will eventually loosen up tight spots in the body structure and increase the body's flexibility.

Healthy Physique

This means more than not being obese or frail. It means that the body is shaped to optimize health, given the genes. A healthy body should have adequate mass to protect its vital organs and functions but should not have excessive mass that burdens these vital organs and functions. The Center for Diseases Control (CDC) has established that the body mass index (BMI) for a normal healthy adult is between 18.5 and 22.0.

The movements of Tai Chi and Aikido even strive for a higher goal than physical health, that of inner peace. A condition of inner peace is internal balance, which is reflected outwardly by a balanced physique. A proven principle of self-transformation is that we become what we focus on. In other words, if we focus on inner peace, our mental body, energetic body and physical body will align and adjust to support that goal. If we constantly reinforce that internal focus by repeating certain exercises designed to achieve this goal, over time our body will change to support the goal.

In particular, the physical body will shed extra mass or build up mass to provide the optimum support to our goal of reaching internal balance and inner peace. In the long run, Aikido and Tai Chi will help a student lose weight if that weight interferes with the student's drive to achieve peace; or gain mass if the student is too frail to reach balance and peace. But it is a gradual process that will take time.

In conclusion, physical fitness is an incidental result of training in Aikido and Tai Chi. However, this transformation will not be as quick as dieting to lose weight, but takes place at the same rate as the overall transformation of the person, with each body - spiritual, mental and physical - transforming itself in harmony with the others.

March 11, 2005

22

Square Pegs, Round Holes

Our oldest son was entering the junior year of high school and our family had begun the task of preparing him for the college process. Parenting two active teenager boys, holding down a full-time professional job and running a dojo at the same time, even with my wife's help, have contributed to my occasional feeling that I was forcing square pegs into round holes around me. Fortunately Aikido and Tai Chi came to the rescue.

Our daily life consists of a series of interactions with our environment. We receive information from our environment, process it and act in a certain way. For this discussion, information refers to every bit of data that we receive pertaining to the people and things around us. In this interaction, we often have a dilemma. On the one hand, "Did I consider all the information that I should before I decide and act?" and on the other hand, "Did I take in too much information and not act decisively or timely enough?"

For example, when you have to choose among competing options for how to spend your Saturday afternoon (attend a niece's graduation upon her insistence, train at an Aikido seminar as advised by your sensei, or listen to your tired body and rest and recover from a busy week of work) what and how many factors do you consider before deciding on an action? If you are a goal-driven type of person, it won't take you long to decide, but are you sure that you have considered all relevant factors and made the right decision? If you are the thoughtful or sentimental types you'll weigh many factors (your relationship to your niece, your respect for your sensei, your health condition, etc.) and hold off as long as you can until one of these factors emerges as the deciding factor and a decision appears for you.

The art of living consists of a balance between being sensitive to your environment (people and circumstances) and taking firm action. How much should I yield? How firm should I be? From the internal energy aspect, it is a balance between receiving energies that come to you and discharging your energy in a focused manner toward a goal. In other words, you need to be sensitive to all things around you without losing your focus in life.

We practice this balancing skill in Aikido training, receiving the *nage's* energy appropriately, re-aligning our energy with it and redirecting it to a neutral target. If we receive too much we'll become overly passive and possibly overwhelmed and our technique would lack clarity and resolution. If we don't receive enough it would be difficult to achieve harmony in movement and we would give the impression that we are bulldozing our way through the technique.

The key question is how to be sensitive without being overwhelmed. I will describe three techniques to achieve this balance. For this purpose, we look at human beings as energy clusters of a particular configuration, which coexist with other clusters of various configurations in the universe.

The following three techniques are presented in order of increasing difficulty.

The first technique is to selectively tune out certain external stimuli.

This technique consists of playing deaf ear to selected bits of data that are knocking at the door of your senses as soon as you recognize that it is not something that you want to deal with. The loud music is blaring but you choose to focus on your writing project so you tune the music out. Your child is tugging at you when you walk past the ice cream shop but you choose to complete your errand and ignore his request. Your spouse has been dropping many hints about that romantic getaway but you just take a mental note and go on with other priorities. Your best friend has been reminding you about joining that club that she just started but you have been politely evading her due to time constraint.

This approach requires much discipline. It takes a lot of self-control to let in only the amount of energy that you want to work with and shut the door on the rest. You would have to be constantly on the alert. It is suitable for goal-driven people. However, it does not allow you to harmonize with your total environment, since you are shutting some things out.

The second technique is to dissolve internal energetic blockage.

In this case you are letting in the bits of information without screening them. Once the external energy has penetrated your energetic body, it will meet with your internal energetic configuration, which is reflected in the specific makeup of your physical, mental and spiritual bodies. Trouble starts when there is not a match-up between the external and the internal.

The foreign energies are square pegs and you've got round holes to receive them. Your thirteen-year old daughter begs to stay out until midnight, an unreasonable request in your opinion considering that you were raised on a 10:00 PM curfew schedule. Her constant pleading causes tension because her demand is a form of energy that does not reconcile with your internal energetic make up. If this impasse is not resolved, the involved energies will transmute into emotions that may become trapped inside your body.

During the day your energetic body will be constantly assailed by incompatible energy patterns that tend to clog up your energy channels the way fatty deposits clog up our arteries. At the early stage, when the energy deposits are still unsubstantial, intense and sustained physical activities such as concentrated physical work, sports or martial arts will enhance energy circulation and dislodge these energy clots and drain them out of your system. That is why we feel refreshed after a physical workout. If the clots are not eliminated regularly they will grow and block your internal energy flow to a point of causing mental fatigue or physical discomfort. Then, massage or various manipulation of the body may alleviate blockages.

But the ultimate cure is to dissolve these blockages through internal mental processes such as psychotherapy or Chi Kung. Other internal arts such as Tai Chi, Aikido or Yoga, which facilitate *ki* flow help you to achieve the same release. After the blockages are cleared your mind achieves clarity and you are more in tune with your surroundings and can make sound decisions.

This second technique requires diligent practice since the dissolution of internal energy blockages must be carried out slowly and methodically and sustained over time to achieve safe and effective results.

The third technique is to modify your internal receptors to fit any shape of incoming energy. I am presently far from being proficient in this technique but have sufficient knowledge of its effectiveness to present it here for your consideration.

In this approach, you transform your round hole into an adaptive hole that can take an assortment of pegs. We are referring to a process that makes our internal energetic framework more loose and accommodating. This may be accomplished through self-cultivation, a process that enlarges the sense of self and allows it to connect to a larger network.

Self-cultivation consists of activities that promote the connection of the individual self with its surrounding; or, from the energy aspect, activities that allow one energy cluster to align itself easily with other clusters. Examples are formal education that leads to new understanding and acceptance, or practice of religion that elevates the spirit to higher realms. The ultimate goal is to extend the individual self until it dissolves and merges with the universal spirit. Such merging is the result of complete alignment of energy from the individual cluster with the surrounding clusters.

These practices in effect loosen our internal energy structure and eventually dissolve our core. When that happens, our sense of self is transformed and our perception of the world is radically altered. In this state there is a void in our inner core that can accept foreign energies of all types and shapes. The mind is crystal clear and whatever decision one makes is in harmony with the environment.

A person whose self has been erased in that manner would still live a normal life but would possess infinite tolerance and forbearance. Any incoming energy would go right through them and be dissolved. The round holes are now black holes that can take any peg. O Sensei Morihei Uyeshiba, the founder of Aikido, was such a person. He apparently did not need to execute techniques when faced with adversaries: he just needed to stand and extend his *ki* then they would be sucked into him as into a vacuum.

This third technique is a practice that requires one to devote a lifetime to self-cultivation or more precisely, self-annihilation.

Lao Tzu wrote in the *Tao Te Ching*:

> *Between heaven and earth,*
> *There seems to be a bellows:*
> *It is empty, and yet it is inexhaustible;*
> *The more it works, the more comes out of it.*
> *No amount of words can fathom it:*
> *Better look for it within you.*

September 19, 2005

23

When Am I Ready to Teach?

A very dedicated student ranked Nidan had just left the dojo to relocate to another state in an area with no Aikido dojo in the vicinity. To continue his practice he started teaching classes in a shared martial arts studio. He has been lamenting about how he could not get the same satisfaction from Aikido training as he did when he was with us. He asked for advice on whether he was really ready to teach Aikido.

Over the years Aikido students at different stages in their training have asked me questions about their readiness to teach. Here is a summary of my answers.

First we need to distinguish between "instructing" and "teaching".

For the sake of this discussion, instructing means to give out objective instructions to help someone execute a task or technique. An instructor "instructs" students on how to do forward rolls. On the other hand, "Teaching," means to do what it takes to cause a person to grow. O Sensei "taught" Aikido to Saito Sensei for twenty-three years and turned him into a fine teacher.

Instructing is a concrete short-term task whereas the teaching that we are referring to is a long-term involvement. The instructor's goal is to help the student acquire a specific skill or ability. The teacher has the more arduous responsibility of effecting a paradigm shift in his or her students and taking them to the next level of growth. A student-teacher relationship is deep at the guts level and could last a lifetime.

In the context of martial arts, an instructor (*Shidoin*) usually refers to a person who is in charge of conducting classes or carrying out other instructional duties. A teacher (*Sensei*) is usually someone who owns or operates a dojo or a club, or is otherwise wholly responsible for the training needs of a group of students.

Teaching Aikido is a responsibility that no one should take lightly because it concerns directly the welfare of other human beings. It is based on a deep yet fragile trust. The rest of our discussion pertains mostly to the qualifications of the teacher rather than the instructor.

Here is the answer to the question "When am I ready to teach?"

You are ready to teach when you fulfill all of the following conditions:

1. You have a burning desire to share.
2. You believe in what you teach.
3. You have grasped the essence of the art.
4. You can create and maintain a supportive environment to carry on the teaching.

A Burning Desire to Share

You will know when the time is right for you to teach, because you will hear that calling loud and clear from deep inside. Some will hear this calling earlier than others along the Aikido path, depending on the maturity of their soul. At some point along its journey through life the soul needs to reach out to others in order for it to travel further. Knowledge is an accumulative burden that needs to be continually unloaded unto others if the soul is to continue its travel.

The desire to share can be cultivated. Or rather, we can facilitate its surfacing with certain practices of sharing in a nurtured environment. Examples of such practices are: helping others during training, coaching fellow students for their *kyū* tests, offering to take falls for a *sempai*, contributing various services to the dojo or to students. These practices allow the seed of sharing to slowly germinate.

Before anyone can aspire to teach he or she would have practiced plenty of sharing in the dojo and elsewhere. When one is ready to teach one will always put others' growth before one's own quest.

A teacher is also someone who is in charge of his own growth and does not rely on another teacher. This does not mean that one should not have another person guide one's growth. It means that one should be self-motivated and self-reliant during one's own quest while teaching.

Sometime a person is forced by circumstances to "teach" Aikido to others, such as when there is no current teacher to learn from in the vicinity. In this case, even though one is not ready one is forced by circumstances to carry out teaching duties. This precocious teaching can be a double-edged sword. Obstacles will abound. If one overcomes them then the path is much easier when the inner calling is heard. It is similar to taking advanced placement courses in high school to get credit for college. However, if one becomes disheartened from the frustrations of teaching then one would suffer a major setback, which may be demoralizing.

A teacher's commitment to the task will be tested over and over by various trying circumstances such as conflicting priorities, students' personal issues and business challenges. For example, a teacher's mettle will be tested when she builds up a club or dojo from scratch. She will have to hold classes rain or shine, in health or in sickness, four times a week, whether or not any students show up.

Many have failed for lack of perseverance under overwhelming odds. Those who hang on will eventually enjoy the incomparable satisfaction of helping people to find their inner peace. That is the same satisfaction that motivates the old man to build the bridge for the youth who comes after him in the poem "The Bridge Builder" by William Dromgoole.

We should be careful though, to make the distinction between the desire of the soul to share and the desire of the ego to make its mark. In this latter case, the goal is not really to help others grow but to self-aggrandize. Such teachers are mainly interested in displaying their skills rather than reaching out to the students and showing them the path. These individuals may be excellent technicians but poor teachers.

A Firm Belief in the Worthiness of the Path

A teacher treads an arduous path filled with pitfalls, surprises and trials. If he or she is not driven by an unshakable belief in the goodness of the mission then failure is certain. A teacher must to lead with confidence and exude sufficient enthusiasm to inspire students.

Anyone who has attempted to start a club or a dojo knows that this is a thankless task that demands unwavering determination. There are often insurmountable challenges raised by our societal structure that must be overcome. Teaching Aikido is not a mainstream activity in the context of the contemporary American society in which material wealth still dominates the spiritual aspects of life and alternative spiritual paths have no official recognition except as cults.

Teachers who are not well grounded in the path they walk on often have to make compromises to survive as teachers. Such compromises often taint the purity of the path and dilute its worthiness. Some may argue that it is better to advocate a compromised path than not doing anything at all to advance the cause of the art.

For example, some teachers may yield to popular interest or media focus and relegate Aikido to just a self-defense art or a fighting art. They get entangled in the debate about the merit of Aikido techniques versus fighting techniques of other martial arts. This approach will cause these teachers to stagnate at this level and even modify Aikido techniques incorrectly. Other teachers may give in to financial pressures and incorporate popular but non-Aikido activities in the curriculum. These activities will shift the focus of the dojo away from the ideals of Aikido.

A Total Grasp of the Essence of the Art

Someone once told me: "You should know your art inside out, backward and forward before you can attempt to teach it to someone else". You should travel that path daily back and forth and know the twist and turns and pitfalls along the way.

The teacher must reach to the essence of the art and create his personal expression of it rather than paraphrasing others. When a person borrows knowledge and teaches by merely replicating someone else's teachings, she is likely not ready to teach. The borrowed knowledge does not reflect the true person of the teacher and will not ring true to the students.

In addition to its martial nature, Aikido is also a transformational art. A mistake can result in either physical harm or psychological damage. Some damages may be irreparable. For example, if you demand complete trust from your student and you breach it once, you may destroy permanently the student's ability to trust others.

The teacher must be well versed in teaching skill, that is, the skill to cause the student to grow under various circumstances. Sometime a teacher needs to teach in spite of the student's unwillingness to learn. In this case, the teacher needs to know how to set up the student and circumstances such that learning occurs.

In order to foster the growth of each student the teacher must be able to disassemble the elements of the teaching and re-assemble them in a format that is most suitable for each individual to assimilate.

In the long run, as the teaching is transported over times and over geographic areas, the teacher must know what must remain unchanged and what can be changed to adapt to the students and circumstances. For example, not all practices related to Japanese customs in the 1920's are necessary for the proper understanding of Aikido. The teacher must know which to modify and how.

Furthermore, some subjects can only be taught in a covert or indirect way, such as by unspoken examples or by creating relevant experiences. A teacher should be sufficiently creative to embed the essence of the teaching within the example or the experience.

The Ability to Create a Favorable Environment for Teaching

The skilled teacher realizes that he cannot carry on the teaching alone and needs to build a supportive environment. This includes a structured approach such as a well-organized curriculum; a code of etiquette; an organization such as a dojo; membership in an association of peers; and helpers such as *sempai*.

A teacher should be able to design a curriculum that is most appropriate for her student population. Factors to consider are age, gender, education level and demographic attributes.

The teacher should also be able to create and maintain an environment that is most conducive to safe and enjoyable training. This includes establishing an appropriate business organization and class structure.

The teacher must set up an organization such as a club or a dojo, with business rules that support her approach to teaching. This should be set up in a way to attract and retain students from the target group.

The teacher must create a student hierarchy and ranking procedures that reinforce the teaching.

The teacher must affiliate with other teachers, peer groups and associations that promote the teaching.

Someone who is a highly proficient martial artist but possesses weak organizational skill may not become a successful teacher.

In summary, teaching is part of a person's growth and will emerge naturally from his or her training. The above discussion describes the enormous responsibility of a teacher and is not meant to discourage students from aspiring toward a teaching career in Aikido.

On the contrary, training with the personal goal of teaching others is the best way to learn Aikido. Those who envision this path should prepare by enrolling in serious training programs such as *uchideshi*, or instructor certification (*fukushidoin* and *shidoin*). If one stumbles on the teaching path by chance one should decide quickly to either act as a teacher and persevere through a period of on-the-job teacher's training or get out and return to a student role. It would be an untenable position to be an unwilling teacher.

In teaching you must give a lot, but you also get plenty of returns.

December 2, 2005

24
Kihon Waza

Around 2005 I worked with other members of the board of directors of the Takemusu Aikido Association to update the ranking requirements for the association. As we went through the requirements for the dan ranks I realized that we did not have a common understanding or definition of certain key terms used in the requirements, such as kihon waza. I wrote this explanation below.

Kihon waza means basic techniques. Proficiency in *kihon waza* is required for the rank of *shodan*.

Kihon waza refers not only to the way a technique is executed but also to a group of core techniques.

The core techniques include *ikkyo, iriminage, shihonage, kokyuuho, kotegaeshi, nikyo, sankyo, yonkyo, kokyunage* and *koshinage*. These are the techniques that define Aikido. All serious students of Aikido must study these well.

When training in *kihon waza* the technique is stripped down to the bare essentials and must be executed slowly and one step at a time. Speed and power are initially not part of execution so that the student can concentrate exclusively on the correct form.

In *kihon waza* the technique is broken down into its component steps, usually four or five. *Shomenuchi iriminage* for example, contains five steps: (1) Extend arm up to meet with *uke's* arm; (2) Enter behind *uke* and turn to align body in *hanmi*

AIKIDO INSIGHTS

in the same direction as *uke's*; (3) Bring *uke* into our alignment by grabbing his collar and cutting downward, locking his head into our shoulder; (4) Take *uke* into a new direction by turning our hips and catching his chin in an upward circular extension of our arm; (5) Step forward and throw.

With numerous repetitions of the correct form, the student builds a basic template of the technique within herself. When this basic mold is firmly assimilated, then other elements such as power (*kokyu*), speed, timing and angles can be added to suit the circumstances.

It is similar to learning to write by hand-printing letters of the alphabet one stroke at a time before you write with cursive and venture into calligraphy.

Besides learning the correct form, there are other benefits of training in *kihon waza*.

Since *kihon waza* focuses on the essential elements, the student learns to do only the bare minimum, that is, without extraneous movements. In this way the student performs the technique efficiently, with no wasted motion. Efficiency is a key goal of martial arts.

Additionally, when advanced students return frequently to *kihon waza* they reinforce the base which supports their effort to reach *takemusu aiki*, the ideal of Aikido training. A solid base is similar to a strong root system that allows a tree to grow vigorously and thrive. As these advanced students become more proficient and start to experiment and develop their own styles, the practice of *kihon waza* will help them to recognize the boundaries of Aikido and recognize movements and concepts that are extraneous to Aikido. In this way they will keep their experimentation within the realm of Aikido.

Another benefit for advanced students is that continuous reinforcement of the basics allows them to communicate their understanding with clarity to beginners. This firm grasp of the basics facilitates their teaching tasks.

In the long run, *kihon waza* training maintains the integrity of Aikido and helps us to perpetuate it for future generations.

March 12, 2006

25

Yawarakai Waza

This was part of my effort to elucidate some of the key terms used in the dan rank requirements for the Takemusu Aikido Association.

Yawarakai waza literally means gentle techniques and refers to the manner the technique is executed. It is a requirement for the rank of *nidan* in our dojo.

Yawarakai is the next level of practice after several years of work on *kihon waza*. Gentle in this context means not hard as in the *kihon waza* but also not yet flowing as in *kinonagare waza*.

It emphasizes curvilinear and continuous motion as different from the more linear and segmented execution in *kihon waza*.

For example, the *kihon* form of *shomenuchi iriminage* consists of five steps: (1) Extend arm up to meet with *uke's* arm; (2) Enter behind *uke* and turn to align body in *hanmi* in the same direction as *uke's*; (3) Bring *uke* into our alignment by grabbing his collar and cutting downward, locking his head into our shoulder; (4) Take *uke* into a new direction by turning our hips and catching his chin in an upward circular extension of our arm; (5) Step forward and throw.

In *yawarakai* form, this same technique is executed in a continuous motion that includes smooth transitions between the five steps, at slow to medium speed and little *kokyū* power. The focus is on the flow.

AIKIDO INSIGHTS

The assumption is that the student is already proficient with the correct form, the correct angle and the proper *kokyū* after having gone through the *kihon waza* stage. If there is any doubt or gap in this proficiency, then more *kihon waza* is prescribed.

Using the art of writing as an analogy, *kihon waza* would be the practice of tracing the different strokes of a letter of the alphabet by hand until they represent the correct printed form of the letter. *Yawarakai* writing would be to link the strokes and the letters and let them flow into one another as you trace them to form a word, as in cursive handwriting.

If the writer has not yet achieved proficiency in *kihon*, that is, have the ability to write each letter in its correct form, and yet moves on to *yawarakai* at an early stage, the cursive handwriting may be hardly legible.

Similarly in Aikido, the student who has not grasped the basics of *iriminage* will have a problem in performing the technique in *yawarakai* format. For example, he may not turn the hips sufficiently to blend in the direction of the *uke's* strike, or fail to bring *uke* into his alignment before turning for the throw.

As a general rule, students should focus on *kihon waza* through the *shodan* rank, then begin to explore *yawarakai waza* thereafter. However, in classes in which ranks are mixed, the training is conducted at the common denominator. Therefore, students should find time outside of the regular class to do personal training and work on their particular needs. In that regard, ten minutes of additional training after formal class will go a long way.

June 26, 2006

26

Forty-year Lessons

On January 2, 2007 I celebrated the completion of forty years of training in Aikido with a seminar at which I shared five important discoveries along my journey. I am exposing them again here with the hope that they may serve as beacons to guide others on the Aiki path.

A life experience often does not become a lesson until after it is learned. In other words one does not realize the value of the experience until hindsight. During the experience itself it is mostly hard work, and one forges ahead simply because one has faith in those who have gone ahead.

Well, as one who has treaded the path before many of you I can assure you that there are immensely valuable lessons to be harvested along the path in front of you. I am sharing here some that have accrued to me.

Just reading them will not do much for you except provide some temporary mental stimulation. You need to train hard, stop and reflect on your experience in the context of these principles, make adjustments then repeat this sequence ad infinitum.

Here are the lessons that I learned, in the order that they came to me.

1. The most efficient movement originates from the hips, the seat of *Kokyu*.

The hips here refer to the waist area (*koshi*) that has at its center what is known as *hara*. The *hara* is the store of *ki* in the body. This principle is based on the premise that Aikido as a martial art seeks to achieve efficiency of movement, that is, use as little energy as possible to achieve a desired impact. Since the seat of our energy is in the hips, the secret of energy efficiency is to find the way to connect the hips as directly as possible to the desired outcome. This is done first by connecting the hips to the trunk, then the hips to the limbs, then the hips to any weapon that we hold, then finally the hips to the target. In short, when the movement originates from the hips it can cause the body to move as one unit and deliver the maximum flow of energy with minimal leakage toward the target. The early years of training will require maintaining a rigid relationship among the body parts (hands, hips, feet, etc.). Afterwards, when the energy has found the most efficient path, the martial artist can relax the body and achieve the same efficiency. This secret, though described explicitly here, can only be unlocked by assiduous training.

2. Aikido energy follows spirals: outward and inward.

Energy transmits in spirals in nature. Aikido movements are in harmony with natural movements and therefore follow spirals. In fact, energy moves only in spirals. Some human movements reflect these spirals better than others if they are tuned into them. A human movement is made up of several layers of energy enveloping a core that is a spiral. If all the layers conform tightly to the core then the spiral manifests outwardly. This is what most students should aim for. Years later, upon mastery of the internal energy, the spiral can be intentionally hidden under loose layers until close to the final impact. In that way, a seemingly innocuous move can deliver a very focused spiral that may not be seen but can definitely be felt by the receiver.

3. The technique happens as you want it: you create it with your intent then let it manifest.

We live in an energy matrix with criss-crossing energy lines. The Creator has pre-configured some of these energy lines into shapes that are inanimate objects or sentient beings. Humans are endowed with a bit of this creative power in the guise of "intent". A human being can re-arrange the energy lines around him/her with his/her intent. The intent generates a conceptual sketch (an idea) that will materialize in specific forms that help to support the idea. The seasoned martial artist would concentrate on the idea instead of the form. Attachment to specific forms puts unnecessary restrictions on the way the idea manifests and may not result in the desired outcome.

This principle also contains one of the most important precepts of martial arts: you can create the situation that you want to be in. In other words, you do not react to a situation but you take the initiative and create the optimal conditions for your technique to express itself.

As an application, in a *randori* (multiple attacks) or *jiyu-waza* (free style) situation a good strategy for the defender is not to try to decide quickly on the appropriate technique to counter each attack but to focus his intent on the desired outcome, which may be "get out of harm". The more advanced martial artist can choose the idea "get out of harm using Aikido techniques and without harming others" and let his training experience take over to achieve the desired outcome.

4. We are all in it together: approach your training partner not with the intent of destroying him but with the intent of restoring his wholeness.

Most people will look at this approach as a radical way of dealing with aggression. It is almost the "turn the other cheek" approach. This is the hallmark character that differentiates Aikido from other martial arts. The purpose of doing Aikido is to restore balance, not to annihilate the source of discord or violence.

We should realize that whatever we do to the other person will come back to us because of our energetic inter-connection with that person. In a conflict we understand that the aggressor is a member of our Family who has temporarily lost his balance. We use Aikido to help that person regain his balance and thus preserve the integrity of our Family. When we train in Aikido with the mindset that there is no enemy and that the aggressor is part of the family, this attitude will be reflected in the type and quality of the techniques.

5. Unlock the Aikido essence within you: it's already inside you by divine design, all you need to do is to tune in with the divine key to unlock this essence and let it manifest as *Takemusu Aiki*.

In other words, Aikido exists already in its pure form within each of us. We need only to rediscover it by removing the obstacles that stand in the way of its manifestation. This is a realization that came late in my martial art career and I have no adequate words to fully explain it yet. I would just invite you to keep training until this meaning is revealed to you directly.

April 1, 2007

27

Women in Aikido

One day I answered the dojo phone and a male caller said that he was interested in Aikido but heard that it is more suited to women and wanted to know whether that was true. I told him that Aikido is useful for everyone but it is also correct to say that it is more suitable for women than other high-impact martial arts. I either confused him or gave him something to think about. I do not remember the rest of our conversation but here are my thoughts on this subject.

Irrespective of what social norms and science say about the subject, I have observed that, based on my thirty-year teaching experience, men and women approach Aikido differently. It is my belief that, in order for members of either sex to attain the best that Aikido can offer, each person needs to absorb and express Aikido according to his or her innate abilities.

At the physical level, men tend to express power through their techniques and usually enjoy a hard physical workout. Women use more suppleness in their techniques and often enjoy the interaction with their training partners more than the reward of physical exertion.

At the mental level, most men are attracted to the rigid discipline and code of etiquette of the martial art and most also thrive on some sort of competition, either implicitly against the training partner or quietly against the self, since Aikido does not promote open competition. Women, on the other hand, care more about the quality of their interaction with their training partner, especially in the aspects of trust and commitment.

These are general observations which do not apply to every student of Aikido but which are helpful to note and understand in order to maximize the benefit of training. My views are derived from the vantage of an experienced teacher of the art. However, they may contain limitations and flaws that I am willing to correct based on new authentic experience or validated observations.

Although I have made the above distinction between the physical and the mental aspects of Aikido training for purpose of explanation, the following discussion is based on the total experience since Aikido is a holistic art that uses the physical to affect the mental and create the spiritual.

I observe that women who thrive in Aikido capitalize on their feminity while conforming to the power-based and rigid methods of men.

Here is a closer look at one aspect of this feminine approach. In the *kihon waza* practice of the Iwama style of Aikido, a firm grip and solid stance are essential for learning the techniques. The purpose of the firmness is not to build physical strength – although it does – but to elicit the use of focused intent in executing the technique. Male students may misunderstand this purpose and apply power inappropriately. Whereas, when faced with an *uke* who squeezes her arm to the degree of blocking any further motion, the woman would calmly tell her *uke* to back off slightly so that she can proceed with the technique. In the same situation a male student is more likely to get excited in the struggle to overcome the opposing force. Requesting his *uke* to downshift would hurt his ego and make him feel inadequate. The misguided male student may then look to power training to enhance his technical performance.

Another physical aspect of feminity is seen in the use of the hips: the female student is more likely to rely less on upper body strength and more on her hips to execute technique. This is certainly a superior strategy in Aikido training that the male students do not readily acknowledge, especially in the context of the Iwama style of Aikido which requires regular use of arm strength at least in the early stage of training.

During interaction with a training partner the typical male student is more concerned about completing the technique in the most effective manner, through use of speed and power. The female student would pay more attention to certain non-physical qualities of the interaction, such as the level of trust and care. A woman would want to know about her training partner and would note whether her training partner care about her safety or about her emotional state. If she detects a disregard of her welfare, the woman may not feel connected to the partner and may decide not to continue the interaction, either bowing out or shunning this training partner in the future.

A male student who acknowledges the natural expression of feminity from his female training partner is likely to get her total engagement and the resulting satisfaction of a deep and meaningful connection throughout the technique.

The female students have a natural need to reach out to other people that is often not recognized by a male teacher. Whereas a male student can join the dojo and train diligently without much interpersonal relation with his training partners other than the physical action on the mat, a female student wants to know her training partners more intimately as people. Therefore, the women in a dojo are encouraged in their training when there are opportunities to socialize and interact with other dojo members outside of the mat.

From a technical standpoint, female aikidoists are more at ease during *jiyuwaza* and *randori* training than their male counterparts. Their fluid energy and intuitive expression prefer the uninterrupted and instinctive flow of these types of practices to the fragmentation and rigidity associated with *kihon waza*. We should remember that, in the continuum of training levels, we practice *kihon waza* to progress to *yawarakai waza* and move on to *kinonagare* waza in which the *ki* flows freely. In this regard, if one's *ki* is already naturally fluid and un-impeded by the ego-mind, then it would be somewhat counterproductive to put too much emphasis on rigid *kihon waza* training. Thus, it may not be beneficial for all women to spend the same amount of time and effort on *kihon waza* as the male students.

The above observation should not be construed as a denial of the importance of *kihon* training. It is part of the training continuum of a time-tested system. Any serious student should learn the complete continuum to be able to teach the art later. What we are saying is that not everyone needs to begin at the same starting point, spend the same amount of time at each training stage or adopt the same tools in order to reach the ultimate training goal.

I have constantly noted that although there are fewer female students, they tend to stick around longer than the average male students and become more ardent supporters of the art. In other words, once a female student has made up her mind about Aikido as her chosen path, she makes a commitment that is not easily matched by most male students. The modern-day dojo should provide more opportunities for women to make this commitment.

It is my view that the current training framework in many Aikido dojos does not provide sufficient encouragement to the female population. This framework has worked well to promote the growth of Aikido in more structured and traditional societies as in Japan and has produced many excellent proponents of the arts, mostly male. For Aikido to serve the totality of humankind, the establishment as well as individual teachers should shed their gender-biased methods and adopt a more flexible teaching model. While remaining anchored in the essence of the art, this model should create an environment in which women can build on their innate strengths and capitalize on their instinctive tendencies in their endeavor to reach *Takemusu Aiki*, the ultimate communion with the universe.

November 23, 2008

28

Ranks in Aikido

As I was compiling the list of candidates for the next kyū exams in the dojo, it occurred to me that although I have always encouraged students to constantly train for their next test, I have not sufficiently explained the reason and consequently students may place undue importance on ranks.

Going through the ranks is an integral part of the Aikido experience. An adult student typically begins at the rank of 6th *kyu* and undergoes a series of exams during the next three to five (four on average) years of training to get to the end of 1st *kyu*. Thereafter one takes the exam for the rank of *shodan* (translated as "beginning grade"), also known as black belt first degree. The *kyu* grades are in effect a countdown to the rank of *shodan*. In this way the first four years of Aikido training in *kyu* grades are viewed as preparatory training for the journey that begins with *shodan*. Thereafter, one progresses through the ranks of *nidan* (2nd degree), *sandan* (3rd degree), *yondan* (4th degree), etc. The top dan grade of *judan* (10th degree) is held only by a handful of people in the world who are outstanding exponents of the art. This journey can take several decades and last till the end of our life.

The rank of *shodan* thus denotes a significant threshold indicating that the student is now ready to receive, or be deserving of, the full Aikido teaching. In other words, *shodan* is when one begins the study of Aikido in earnest.

In the old times, Japanese martial arts students did not get ranks. Typically, after having unloaded his complete teaching unto the student the teacher would award him a teaching license (*menkyo kaiden*) certifying that the holder is qualified and authorized to teach the art. Some schools still operate on this *menkyo* method. This system worked when life was simple. In a modern lifestyle students are faced with many choices and need a form of recognition to reinforce their commitment to the art. The *kyu-dan* ranking system originated from the art of *Go* and was applied to martial arts and popularized by the late Jigoro Kano, founder of *Kodokan* Judo in the 1880's.

Kyu rankings are administered independently by each dojo-cho (head of the dojo). The dojo-cho has complete discretion in awarding the *kyu* ranks. In some dojos, *kyū*-rank holders may be differentiated by the color of the belt. In others, all *kyū*-rank students wear a white belt.

Dan ranks, on the other hand, are awarded by the Aikikai, the worldwide aikido association led by the *Doshu* (leader of the Way), who is currently the grandson of the Founder. The Aikikai awards the rank based on a certification of examination or a recommendation by an Aikikai-recognized dojo-cho or *kaicho* (leader of an association).

Dan ranks may be issued by other Aikido organizations not affiliated with the Aikikai, which are led by a *soke*, the headmaster of the style. One such *soke* who is relevant to our lineage is Hitohiro Saito Sensei, son of the late Morihiro Saito, the leader of what has been commonly referred to as Iwama style Aikido. It should be noted that the late Saito Sensei always insisted that he taught only what he learned from O Sensei, the Founder. Therefore, in his view, there is no Iwama style, but only O Sensei's Aikido. Although Morihiro Saito Sensei did create the Iwama Ryu ranking system for various reasons in Europe, he always promoted and respected the Aikikai ranking. However, after his passing, the younger Saito Sensei decided to secede from the Aikikai organization and form his own Shin Shin Aiki Shurenkai with his own *dan* rank system.

The first four years of training may not appear significant when one reviews a 40 year training career in Aikido, but they are truly the most important years, similar to the first five formative years of a child. During this *kyu* grade period the student learns all the basic techniques and principles that serve as the foundation for advanced training. The advanced training is only as good as the foundation. Unfortunately, there are no standards for this essential basic training. Hombu Dojo, the headquarters of the Aikikai, does not prescribe standards but issues guidelines for rankings with scant illustration of standard techniques. In the 1970's the late Saito Sensei published a series of five books describing the traditional techniques of Aikido. This was the first authoritative and comprehensive publication of any technical standards. Saito Sensei refreshed this series with a new seven-volume version in the 1990's entitled *Takemusu Aikido*. Then, a few years ago, the current *Doshu* authored his own series of books aimed at filling this gap at the Aikikai.

In 2001 when the Takemusu Aikido Association (TAA) was founded following Saito Sensei's urging before his demise, I helped craft the Ranking Policy of the Association which applies to all member-dojos. This policy is designed to guide students' training to achieve ranks awarded by the Aikikai while also maintaining the specialty of our lineage. Eventually these ranking requirements will lead the dedicated students to the ultimate state of *Takemusu Aiki*.

On a day to day basis, students should refer often to the ranking requirements as a blueprint for their training plans. Students should always train for their next rank. The emphasis is not so much on the end result, the rank, but on the contents of the training. Ranks exist for three main reasons. The primary reason is to provide a methodic approach to training so that a student can take personal responsibility for her growth. Going to class regularly is a necessary but not sufficient condition for proficiency in Aikido. The student should review the ranking requirements and determine her own training needs, then work on them in addition to attending classes. Such personal training can take place during open mat times or other available times before and after classes.

The second reason to have ranks is to provide for an orderly framework for learning. Ranks create a hierarchy which is consistent with the way knowledge and skills are passed on in traditional societies. The basic tenet for learning is that your *sempai* leads the way and you learn by following his/her example or instructions without question. This rule simplifies the learning process and provides an orderly environment for training in the dojo. However, to accommodate the questioning western mind, the rule has been relaxed considerably in most contemporary dojos in the West. Students still have to follow the seniors' examples and instructions but only in the dojo, and they can ask questions.

The third raison d'être for the ranking system is to provide a systematic way for preserving and transmitting Aikido. For instance, if the key elements of *bukiwaza* are not incorporated in the ranking requirements, the weapon system of Aikido may not be completely preserved or properly transmitted. Furthermore, to be effective, learning needs to occur in a particular sequence; that is, students should first become proficient in the *ken suburi* before learning the *kumitachi*; the basic *kumitachi* forms should be mastered before attempting the *henka* (variations).

On the minus side, the ranking system has undesirable by-products. One is the excessive focus on the rank itself and the associated status. When the focus is shifted away from the training and toward the rank, the student's progress is misguided. The student may take certain action that would win him a promotion but would be detrimental to his growth. For example, he may decide to leave a strict teacher to affiliate with another school for a faster track to the next promotion.

The other by-product is the tendency to associate rank with proficiency level. This is not usually an issue at the *kyu* or lower *dan* ranks but there is a discernible problem at the higher rank levels, say from *yondan* on. The problem stems from the fact pointed out earlier that there are no uniform and specific criteria for awarding *dan* ranks. Each teacher and organization may develop their own. Some organizations may put more weight on technical proficiency than others; some may emphasize contribution (service or monetary) to the organization; and some may focus heavily on the development of the art. The discrepancies in ranking criteria may be imperceptible at the lower ranks but become more noticeable at the higher ranks. So, not all *godan* are equal in all respects.

Ranks exist for very practical reasons but their ultimate purpose is to facilitate learning. Let us keep this firmly in mind lest ranks become our ultimate training goals. Let's not train for the ranks but use the rank requirements to train.

May 7, 2009

29

The Mystery of Basics

We held kyū tests recently and I noticed that some students lacked grounding; the "basics" just weren't there. I knew that it was time to refresh interest in that dull practice called "basic". This time, though, instead of lecturing on the benefit of drilling the basics with added urgency as I used to do in the past, I thought it more important to provide a clear explanation of how this benefit is realized. I hope that this understanding will help the students to motivate themselves instead of relying on the teacher's urging.

Much has been said about the importance of basic drills in martial art training. It is a trademark of the Iwama style of Aikido as taught by the late Saito Morihiro Sensei. Saito Sensei's emphasis on training in basic techniques is legendary. He devoted a great portion of his teaching time to basics, repeating ad infinitum the key points of the basic form of every technique. Every one of his students would remember the phrase "drop your elbow, your shoulder and your hips; let your *kimochi* (feeling) sink; turn and look in the same direction as your *uke*" that pertains to *morotedori kokyuho* in every class. It is the same form with the same pointers in every class, be it a regular class or a class in a seminar.

Some in the Aikido community regarded him as an expert technician who cares mostly about how Aikido techniques look and who dwells on the physical aspect of Aikido while ignoring its deeper spiritual underpinnings. It is accurate to say that Saito Sensei emphasized the correctness of the form. But he also has outlined a path that leads from the detailed form through the gradual disappearance of form and ultimately to *Takemusu Aiki*, the state in which the person acts in spontaneous harmony with the surroundings. It was Saito Sensei's view that you train the spirit by first training the body.

There are many who are attracted to Aikido because of its philosophical appeal and who focus heavily on the mystical content at the detriment of the technical clarity of Aikido training. This approach may benefit students who have reached a certain level of spiritual maturity through some other disciplines prior to coming to Aikido. Aikido as created by O Sensei is a martial art that begins with strict and rigorous physical training.

Understanding how a concrete form leads one to spiritual achievement is crucial to the propagation of Aikido as a martial art of peace.

For the sake of brevity many concepts are oversimplified in the following explanation.

In the process of learning a particular form our attention and energy are focused on solidifying the form. We do this by adding incremental detail to the form. More detail adds to the solidity of the form. When the form is built out it contains the maximum level of detail and reaches maximum clarity. At that time the energy that was used to build the detail of the technique is no longer needed at the physical level. Therefore, it is rechanneled to a different aspect of the training, at a more subtle level.

Not too many people achieve this level of clarity in a technique. Most would not have the discipline to get past 60-70% clarity; this is a point when the casual student feels that he has "learned" the technique and is ready to move on. He is not interested in further repetition of the same form and

The Mystery of Basics

would rather seek different stimuli through a variation or a new technique. The serious student though, will forge on and research the finer detail of the same form to obtain a "higher resolution" technique. When these serious students get close to 100% clarity they find that they can add no more detail to the form. At this stage they hit a plateau and feel that they suddenly either have stopped learning or have nothing else to learn.

The few who persevere past this second threshold will break through and find that they are not interested in any variation of the existing form but find new meaning in experiencing the same old form. They touch on a different dimension of training and begin to sense a common thread between certain techniques. Their attention will now train their energy on finding the connectivity among techniques.

After several years of training at this deeper level these students gradually discover the principles that bind certain techniques. Their attention and energy now soar to a finer level of subtlety.

As the training goes on the experienced student dwells mostly at the energetic level of techniques and certain energy patterns are revealed to her. She is able to recognize the energetic signature of each technique and learns to modify the technique through its energetic imprint. In everyday's parlance we say that the student has got the feel for each technique.

The student continues to improve her skill and gradually acquires the ability to recall a particular feeling and to manifest the associated technique at will. Thus she becomes free of form and her training now consists of training her attention – more specifically her intent – to create energy patterns appropriate to the existing physical circumstances. In terms of mat practice, this means that the student uses her intent to allow the appropriate technique to manifest physically to resolve an oncoming attack. This is the beginning stage of *Takemusu Aiki*.

At this stage of learning the student works in the realm of intent rather than the realm of the manifest. This is where Aikido reveals its spiritual make-up.

In summary, the path from the basics to the spirit begins with a strong focus on form. It progresses through building out the form, consolidating it then transcending it. It requires persistent attention to basic forms. If this persistence is lacking and the student chooses to indulge in the variety of flavors of the forms, none of these varied forms would reach sufficient maturity to propel the student to the next level.

For example the *ken suburi* No. 1 is a basic technique of Aikido *bukiwaza*. It appears very simple and uninteresting to the untrained person although it contains a great amount of detail which clearly defines its correct form. The casual student gets quickly bored with this practice and would regard thousand-strike sessions, which used to be staple practice of *uchideshi* of the past, as meaningless torture. On the other hand the serious student who consistently sticks with his daily *suburi* practice and who unceasingly explores the finer detail of this form will realize one day that this *suburi*, as does every basic technique, contains an energetic code which lies at the heart of most Aikido techniques. Continuous and deliberate repetition of the correct form of this *suburi* locks in the form with several layers of energy, from gross to subtle, and at the same time unlocks the code within the technique. This code creates a bridge between the physical form and the layers of energy that allows the student's consciousness to penetrate the depth of the universal *ki* and to reach the source of all techniques.

This is the mystery of basics that ensures that only the dedicated students of martial arts reach the source of all techniques.

From the discussion above one can infer that a person just needs to learn and master one technique in order to reach the source. It is a logical assertion, but who in his right mind would practice just one technique for ten years? Only a person with no-mind (*mushin*) would.

November 2, 2009

30

How Correct Aikido Ukemi Promotes Health

A dedicated student recently injured his toes and had to watch classes from the bench. Someone joked that ukemi was a hazardous activity and he should lay off of it for a while. I knew it was a light-hearted comment but I wanted to correct any possible misconception about ukemi.

In this essay I explain how taking *ukemi* in Aikido can improve your long-term health if done correctly. I will discuss only the physical and energetic aspects, although there are martial, mental and spiritual aspects of *ukemi* that are equally important for Aikido students.

Ukemi is the art of receiving safely the impact of a technique to allow it to run its full course as intended by *nage* (the person executing the technique).

From the viewpoint of physical health there are three types of movement that the *uke* (the person receiving the technique) does that promote health, beside the well-known benefits of aerobic activities such as improved circulation and muscle toning. These three types of movement are: balancing, twisting and tumbling. In the following example we have a female *nage* throwing a male *uke*.

First, what is balancing and how does it promote health? When *nage* executes the technique correctly, *uke's* physical balance is challenged throughout the entire duration of the

155

technique (*kuzushi*), with the result that he is pinned to the ground or thrown away from her. If he takes proper *ukemi*, *uke* would constantly adjust his body so that he remains balanced until the point where he can blend with the ground by either laying flat to absorb a pin or taking a roll. In this way, *ukemi* involves a series of constant postural adjustments to remain aligned with gravity that allow the body to quickly recover from continuing balance upsets caused by the technique. Our Aikido curriculum contains a vast array of techniques that upset *uke's* balance from a multitude of angles, positions and directions, causing him to undergo numerous body adjustments to maintain his balance. Over time, with continuing practice, *uke* increases the coordination among body parts and expands the boundaries of his balance. The improvement in physical coordination and balance results in a safer and healthier interaction with the surrounding world.

The preceding discussion presumes that *nage* executes the technique correctly and that her purpose from the outset should be to upset *uke's* balance with the intent to throw or pin him. If her intent is to create pain or damage his joints then the context is totally different and so should be the *ukemi*. Both *nage* and *uke* need to practice Aikido with the proper intent in order to derive mutual benefit. This is a fundamental tenet of Aikido that should never be forgotten.

Now let's look at twisting. Twisting is often associated with pain in our culture, such as in the phrase "I had him do it after some arm twisting". The pain is there only if you resist the twist. Most Aikido techniques seek to upset the vertical alignment of *uke's* body and/or displace its center. To produce this effect, often a twisting is applied at a peripheral joint (e.g. the wrist in the case of *kotegaeshi* or *nikyo*) or directly at a central joint (e.g. the neck in the case of *kokyuho* or *iriminage*). A skilled *uke* would absorb the spiraling energy from his extremities all the way to his center, that is, allow his muscles and tissues to stretch and let the impact to spread to his entire body from the point of contact through the *hara* (the center of *ki* in the body) in the hips.

For example, in receiving *kotegaeshi* he would relax and let the twisting motion at the wrist cause his forearm to twist until the shoulder joint kicks in and let the entire arm twist. Then the next joint in the sequence, the hip joint, gets to work and prompts the torso to twist to absorb the impact further. The joints at the knee and ankle then begin to feel the twist but they should not be used to absorb the torque; instead *uke* should reposition the entire impacted leg. Through this sequence, the muscles and the related connective tissues (fasciae, ligaments and tendons) are relaxed and get a good dose of stretching as they absorb the energy of the twist. As long as it is not overdone, this stretching strengthens these tissues, improves lymphatic circulation and blood circulation, and increases flexibility.

How can tumbling or rolling bring about any health benefits? One obvious benefit is that the ability to execute a roll on the ground helps one to recover safely following a fall. The lesser known benefit has to do with inversion. During most of our wakeful state we keep an upright posture which is rarely disturbed until we lie down to rest. In this vertical posture the internal organs, especially those in the abdomen, are stacked on top of each other and their surfaces stick with each other. Stickiness reduces plasticity and induces hardening. In addition, sediments including toxic matters are deposited at the bottom of these organs. When we lie down and shift positions there is some relief in the stickiness and some stirring of the sediments.

A sedentary lifestyle exacerbates this stickiness and allows sediments to accumulate, causing sagging organs and increasing the toxicity level. Physical exercises tend to alleviate these conditions, especially those that require twisting motion such as Yoga, Chi Kung, Tai Chi or Aikido. The twisting increases organ muscle tone, strengthen the surrounding tissues and wring out the toxic materials. More helpful are the movements that shake up the organs and turn them upside down during brief moments, such as during a roll.

These moments of inversion cause additional work-out to the muscles and tissues. They also bring the toxic matters in a state of suspension and facilitate their excretion. This is how executing a roll helps to improve our health.

To sum up, Aikido *ukemi* involves three types of movement that can potentially make us healthier: balancing, twisting and tumbling. If not done correctly these movements increase our risk of injury; but when *ukemi* is done properly we become healthier. It pays to be mindful of our *ukemi*.

May 22, 2010

31

First Rei, Then Waza

As I was developing an instructor certification program for our Aikido association I realized that there is no existing material to teach the soft aspect of Aikido, such as the concept and practice of Rei (propriety of conduct). I wrote this essay to fill this gap and concurrently decided that this was the time to put a book together. Hence, this is the last essay in this book.

The first lesson for any student entering a traditional martial arts school is most likely to learn how to perform a proper bow. This bow is the simplest expression and an essential element of *rei*, particularly in the context of a school of Japanese martial art. *Rei* is an integral component of traditional arts, including martial arts.

Rei is both practical and spiritual, taking roots from Confucianism. It is one of the five cardinal virtues that form the foundation of the philosophy expounded by Confucius (551 BCE – 479 BCE): Compassion, Righteousness, Propriety, Wisdom and Trustworthiness.

Rei can be loosely translated as courtesy or propriety, the ability to do the right thing at the right time. *Rei* is the expression of the other four Confucian cardinal virtues through human relations. *Rei* presumes that there is a certain order in the universe that links its various elements in the most harmonious way. In the Confucian cosmology human beings (or men, for brevity) and other creatures of this universe do not exist as separate entities but are interdependent and thrive by relying on each other. Each being in this universe has a duty toward the others. *Rei* acknowledges these relationships and the associated duties that are inherent in this cosmic order and seeks to preserve this order. According to the second law of thermodynamics, energy in the universe tends to move from an orderly state to a state of disorder. It takes a conscious effort to establish and maintain a state of order. *Rei* is that conscious effort. In this discussion we examine *rei* in the context of *budo*.

Any art that involves significant exchanges of energy between men and other elements of the universe (including other men) must necessarily be built on a stable system of relationships among these elements in order for the art to continue to evolve. Without the stability of the relationships the artists would need to divert substantial energy toward the maintenance of relations that could have been used to enrich the art instead. For example, in the case of Japanese martial arts, thanks to the *rei* that exists in the *sempai-kohai* system, the teaching can be transmitted efficiently from *sempai* to *kohai* without being subjected to the distracting interferences of the intellect and personal judgment. The *kohai* is to follow the *sempai* instructions to the letter without questioning. Of course, there are potential flaws that we will address later on.

Rei is at the heart of *budo* and is an integral part of the Bushido code. *Rei* is also what allowed the gradual transformation of *bugei* (fighting arts) into *budo* (martial path) in 17th century Japan. In *bugei*, the *bushi* (warrior) devotes his energy to polish his fighting skill so that he can deal with other men appropriately (kill if necessary). When not fighting, the warriors of old kept their edge sharp by practicing *rei*. As a warrior's practice, *rei* is imbued with the same discipline that is the hallmark of *bushido*. To the *samurai*, the practice of *rei* culminates with the rituals of *seppuku* (cutting the belly) in order to regain the honor that has been lost due to a loss in the battlefield or other failure to uphold the Bushido Code.

First Rei, Then Waza

When the killing and fighting are no longer necessary, the *bushi* diverts more of his energy to polishing other skills to deal appropriately with men. It is this shift that placed higher emphasis on *rei* and caused the birth of *budo*.

In *budo* a simple bow is an acknowledgement by the subject of his relative position and duty in the cosmic order. I bow toward the *shomen* as I enter the dojo to acknowledge that the dojo is a special place in this universe where I train and grow. I bow to O Sensei's picture before a class to signify my readiness to open up and receive his teaching. At the end of class I bow to show gratitude for the spiritual nourishment provided by the art that O Sensei created. I bow to my training partner to acknowledge her special role to help me grow and to request that we begin training together. Each of these bows represents an acknowledgement of a special relationship and its associated duties.

The meaning of the bow represents the content of the *rei* (also referred to as the *ura*, or back). The form of the *rei* (also referred to as the *omote*, or front) has to do with how the bow should be done. The subject should face the object of the bow with an upright posture then deliberately lower the bare head by bending from the waist while keeping the back and head aligned. The positions of the hands and legs depend on whether it is a standing or sitting bow. The deeper the bow, the deeper the acknowledgement and the more special the relationship.

Content reinforces form. *Rei* should be performed with total presence and complete attention to detail, as if this is one's last act on earth. While performing *rei* one's heart must be filled with gratitude and respect toward the person or object of *rei*.

Ideally, the expression of *rei* should be correct as to both form and content. Regrettably, this is not the case in many dojos. We often see students executing the incorrect form of a bow, such as bending at the upper back rather than the waist, or not facing the object of the bow, or without taking off headwear. At other times we see students executing the right form for the bow but without the requisite contents, such as when in a hurry to get to the next action.

Rei, of course, is not just expressed through the bow. *Rei* includes holding proper postures, handling weapons in the proper manner, using the proper words to address people at various levels, speaking at the right time only, wearing the proper attire to a function, presenting the proper gift for the occasion and taking the correct action at the proper time. Below are some examples in an Aikido dojo environment.

With regard to the dojo, *rei* may include the following acts: bowing upon entering and exiting the dojo and the mat area; keeping the facilities clean by keeping shoes on designated racks; keeping the mat clean by keeping hands and feet clean; caring for all things so as to minimize any waste; occasionally bringing flowers or other offerings to the *kamiza*; making a contribution (mat fee or flowers) when visiting a dojo; keeping quiet while watching class in session; refraining from any act that would bring dishonor to the school; etc.

With respect to weapon handling, *rei* may include: treating wooden weapons as live weapons; taking proper care of weapons to prolong their life; giving the weapon the same respect as you would to its owner; etc.

Rei toward one's own body includes taking good care of one's health by exercising moderation and refraining from excesses; keeping proper personal hygiene; wearing the proper attire according to the occasion; maintaining an upright posture; etc.

With regard to fellow students, *rei* may include the following acts: training with anyone who requests of us without personal prejudices; keeping an open mind and learning from all; staying focused and connected with our training partner while executing or receiving techniques; offering generously to help someone in need of guidance; etc.

Rei with regard to a *sempai* may include: receiving instructions and corrections with full attention; expressing thanks when receiving any sort of guidance, whether requested or unwanted; accepting criticism without questions or attempt of rebuttal; giving the right of way to *sempai* (access to the mat, execution of techniques, access to food during a banquet, etc.); always addressing *sempai* with respect; handing over objects with two hands; etc.

Rei with regard to *kohai* may include: accepting total responsibility for mistakes or failures committed by *kohai* while following instructions; putting *kohai's* needs for training before own needs; setting examples by acting first before *kohai*; ensuring the welfare of *kohai*; never abusing a *kohai's* trust; etc.

Rei with regard to sensei may include *rei* accorded to *sempai* supplemented with the following: bowing to greet sensei upon sight; helping with tasks in the dojo; refraining from requesting promotion; properly requesting leave of absence from the mat or from the dojo; requesting prior permission to train when visiting a dojo; keeping sensei informed of important life changes (family, job, sickness); keeping sensei informed of students' needs; etc.

Rei with regard to one's *deshi* (students) may include *rei* accorded to *kohai* supplemented with the following: accepting total responsibility for *deshi's* growth; accepting responsibility for *deshi's* behavior at other dojos; staying aloof of personal relationship with any *deshi*; etc.

Rei toward the Aiki path may include: protecting the integrity of the teaching; disseminating the teaching; refraining from behavior and acts that would sow discord among followers of the path; etc.

The practice of *rei* requires intense discipline and constant vigilance. Each act of *rei* must be carried out with full intent and awareness. Many of these acts are repeated and often become rituals. The student must remain extremely vigilant so that these acts do not become rote and lose their meaning. For

AIKIDO INSIGHTS

example, at the beginning and end of class, the students line up facing the *shomen* and collect themselves before performing the ceremonial bow. Even though brief, this quiet period should be used to allow one's energy and spirit to settle into the center (*hara*), so that one becomes fully aware and present, while waiting for the instructor's cue to perform the bow.

Rei should emanate from the heart and not be dictated by entrenched forms and customs. We learn *rei* first by practicing the form until it becomes second nature, and more importantly, we should understand its underlying meaning and absorb it into our heart. It takes only a few days for a beginning student to learn how to perform a proper bow and say *onegai shimasu* to her training partner, but it may take her several months or years to understand the meaning of that act of *rei* and to allow it to reach her core. Once *rei* has been assimilated through conscious practice, as soon as the student locks eyes with her *uke*, a sense of gratitude will arise naturally and an unspoken and respectful request to train will emanate simultaneously with her bow and the vocalization of the words *onegai shimasu*.

Rei is not fixed. It manifests differently under different circumstances; it should be adapted to the social, environmental, political and historical contexts. *Rei* is expressed differently in feudal Japan and in modern Japan; in Japan and in America; in a warm climate and in a cold climate; in a repressive society and in a liberal society. *Rei* needs to adapt so that it remains alive and ready to guide men toward harmonious co-existence with all creatures.

In the government there are books of protocols; in the military there are books of regulations; in society there are books of etiquette; in Bushido there is *Hagakure* (a.k.a. the Book of the Samurai) that can be helpful to practitioners of modern *budo*. All these publications make recommendations for the correct comportment at specific times, places and occasions. However, they do not cover all situations in life. There are many times when one must decide on the right behavior on the fly by drawing from the depth of one's heart. If *rei* has been absorbed into the heart then the correct action will be clear; if *rei* has not reached the heart, then confusion, faux-pas, misunderstanding and conflict ensue.

Viewed in this light, *rei* is an essential aspect of our Aikido training. It takes on more importance as one promotes through the ranks. At the beginning of our martial art training, we are introduced to *rei* but we normally spend most effort learning *waza* (techniques). During our training journey, *rei* will nurture *waza* through maturity in a few years or decades, but *rei* training endures past this period and will continue to forge our spirit and guide us to ultimate harmony with the universe. *Rei* deserves our constant and increasing attention.

June 29, 2010

AIKIDO INSIGHTS

Epilogue

I hope that some of the concepts and ideas presented in the foregoing essays have stimulated the readers' thinking about Aikido and about their own practice. I assert no claim of originality on these thoughts and concepts. They are mere discoveries along my training journey and reflect my own limited understanding of the nature of Aikido and related arts.

I invite readers to build on these thoughts and use them as stepping stones on the training path. In addition to exploring the practical applications of these ideas, I encourage readers to engage in a serious quest to discover new insights on Aikido and record their findings along the way. This mental activity will enrich their mat training.

Train hard, explore and enjoy.

Gambatte kudasai!

AIKIDO INSIGHTS

Glossary of Japanese Terms

Atemi	Strike to vital points on the body
Budo	Martial ways; refers to martial arts such as, Aikido, Judo, Kendo etc.
Bugei	Fighting arts
Bujutsu	Martial techniques
Bukidori	Techniques for taking away weapons
Bukiwaza	Weapon techniques. In Aikido this refers to practice with the bokken (wooden sword) and jo (staff)
Dojo	Training hall
Dojocho	Chief instructor; headmaster
Doshu	Leader of the Way
Feng shui	Chinese for wind and water; refers to the art of geographical placement to harmonize with the environment
Fuku shidoin	Assistant instructor
Gasshuku	Training camp
Gambatte kudasai	Do your best; best wishes on your endeavor
Giri	Obligation; one of the five cardinal virtues in Confucianism
Godan	Fifth-degree black belt
Hakama	Type of Japanese loose trousers with the look of a long skirt.

Hanmi	Half stance; refers to triangular stance which is characteristic of Aikido
Happo giri	Eight-direction cut
Hara	Center of a person's energy located in the belly, also called tanden
Henka	Variation (of a technique)
Irimi	Type of movement that involves a straight entry
Iriminage	Throw using irimi
Judan	Tenth-degree black belt
Jiyu waza	Free-style technique
Kaicho	Head of association
Kamiza	Altar (for the spirit)
Ken suburi	Refers to a set of basic exercises for the bokken
Ki	Life force
Kiai	Refers to a shout uttered to focus energy
Kihon waza	Basic techniques
Kimochi	Feeling
Ki no nagare	Blending with ki; refers to flowing techniques based on ki blending
Kohai	Junior student
Kokyu	Breath power; refers to extension of ki while executing technique
Kokyuho	A technique using kokyu
Kotegaeshi	A technique involving twisting the wrist
Kototama	Spiritual practice based on sacred

Glossary of Japanese Terms

	sounds
Kumitachi	Paired practice involving swords
Kuzushi	Principle of taking balance
Kyu	Grade; rank before the dan rank
Menkyo kaiden	Teaching certificate
Morotedori	A type of grab using both hands to hold one wrist.
Nage	Person doing the throw
Nidan	Second-degree black belt
Nikyo	Second technique also known as kote mawashi
Onegai shimasu	I request the favor of . . .
Randori	Multiple attacker practice
Rei	Propriety of conduct; refers to one of the five cardinal virtues of Confucianism
Samurai	Warrior class in feudal Japan
Sandan	Third-degree black belt
Sempai	Senior student
Sensei	Teacher
Seppuku	Suicide by cutting through own belly; also known as hara kiri
Shidoin	Instructor
Shodan	First-degree black belt
Shomen	Front; refers to front of dojo where the spirit resides (Kamiza) and to which students bow upon entering dojo

Shomenuchi	Strike to the face
Shuren	Arduous work/training
Suwari waza	Techniques done on knees from a seated position
Tai no henko	Refers to a type of basic turning movement to blend with an attack
Takemusu aiki	Refers to the ideal of Aikido training at which level techniques come forth spontaneously from the source of creation
Tenkan	Refers to a circular blending motion
Uchideshi	Live-in apprentice
Uke	Person taking fall in a technique
Ukemi	Art of taking fall (receiving technique)
Yawarakai waza	Soft techniques; refers to a mode of execution of technique based on soft motion

About the Author

H. Hoa Newens Sensei is the chief instructor of Aikido Institute Davis in California. He has trained and taught Aikido since 1967 and is ranked black belt 6th degree by World Headquarters. Throughout the years, he studied with Dang Thong Phong Sensei, 6th dan, the late Seiichi Sugano Shihan, 8th dan, and the late Morihiro Saito Shihan, 9th dan. Newens Sensei is a former head instructor at Aikido Institute Oakland. He currently serves on the board of Takemusu Aikido Association, a non-profit corporation dedicated to promoting Aikido throughout the world. He has also trained in Wu Tai Chi and Chi Kung since 1987. Newens Sensei has published a comprehensive series of Aikido DVDs entitled Aikido Curriculum, consisting of seven professionally produced DVDs.

Aikido Institute Davis
638 Cantrill Drive, Suite B
Davis, California 95618, U.S.A.
www.aikidodavis.com

Printed in Great Britain
by Amazon